Debrett's Book of the Royal Wedding

DEBRETT'S BOOK OF THE
ROYAL WEDDING

HUGO VICKERS

DEBRETT'S PEERAGE LIMITED

MCMLXXXI

© Hugo Vickers 1981
Introduction © Debrett's Peerage Limited 1981
Published by Debrett's Peerage Limited,
73-77 Britannia Road, London SW6
Distributed by Hamish Hamilton Limited, Garden House,
57-59 Long Acre, London WC2

First published 1981

Designed by Tom Carter and Ian Cameron
Picture research: Philippa Lewis
Caroline Lucas
Penny Davies

Setting by SX Composing Limited, Rayleigh, Essex
Printed by de Lange/van Leer b.v., Deventer, Holland

ISBN 0 905649 35 4

Printed in Holland

Produced by Edition, 25 Lloyd Baker Street, London WC1

Special photography by John N. Sterling: 10; 121a; 125a;
136a, b; 137; 138; 139; 140; 141; 144b

Beedle & Cooper: 166
Camera Press: 9; 13b; 14a,b; 15a; 17; 19b; 23b; 37b; 46; 47; 54; 60; 62; 63;
    69a,b; 73a; 77; 78; 81b; 83; 85; 88; 99; 101a; 104; 107; 117; 120a; 129; 131;
    143; 149a; 150a; 153,b
Camera Press/Peter Abbey: 5; 176
Camera Press/Cecil Beaton: 13a
Camera Press/Colin Davey: 100
Camera Press/Alan Davidson: 156b
Camera Press/Charles de la Court: 155
Camera Press/Peter Grugeon: 113
Camera Press/Karsh of Ottawa: 24a
Camera Press/Lichfield: 116a; 151
Camera Press/David Newall Smith: 145
Camera Press/James Reid: 35
Camera Press/John Scott: 24b; 37b
Camera Press/Richard Slade: 106a
Camera Press/Snowdon: 33; 34; 51b
Camera Press/Snowdon/Vogue: 2
Tim Graham: 125b; 127; 156a; 163; 173
Anwar Hussein: 118a; 119b; 121b; 122a,b,c; 123; 130; 132; 134; 135; 144a
Keystone Press Agency: 7b,c,d; 18a; 18b; 20a,b; 30a; 40; 41; 42; 43; 51a; 66;
    74; 81a; 82; 84; 91; 95; 101b; 103a; 115; 116b; 118b; 124; 126b; 147; 156c;
    157a; 160c; 161a,b,c
Keystone Press Agency/Ian Tyas: 172
National Portrait Gallery, London: 164; 165
Photographers International Ltd: 174
Photographers International/Jayne Fincher: 157b
Photographers International/Terry Fincher: 175
Photographers International/Paul Harris: 162
Popperfoto: 12; 15b; 19a,c; 21a,b,c; 25a,b; 27; 28; 29c; 30b, c; 31; 32; 37a; 38a;
    52; 53; 57; 61; 64; 68a; 72; 73b,c; 75; 79; 87; 90a,b,c; 94; 96; 97; 98; 205;
    114b; 119a; 120b; 148a; 154b
The Press Association: 3; 6; 142; 159; 160a
Sport & General Press Agency: 7a
Syndication International Ltd: 14c; 18c; 22; 23a; 26a; 26b,c; 29a,b; 38b;
    50a; 50b; 55; 58; 59; 68b; 71; 76; 89; 93; 103b; 106b; 108; 109a,b; 110a;
    114a; 128; 148b; 149b; 150b; 152a,b; 154a; 158; 160b
Hugo Vickers: 44; 45; 48; 49; 69c 70; 110b; 111; 126a; 133
Hugo Vickers/Lichfield: 112

Contents

Lady Diana smiling happily on the day of the announcement.

Frontispiece: Lady Diana Spencer photographed in the autumn of 1980 by Lord Snowdon.

Title page: Lady Diana with Prince Charles on their engagement day, 24th February 1981.

Introduction

by
Patrick Montague-Smith
Former editor of Debrett

I cannot think of anyone more suitable to write a book in celebration of the forthcoming Royal Wedding of the Prince of Wales than Hugo Vickers. For many years he has been interested in the Royal Family and has now become a considerable expert. In particular, he has kept a close eye on the busy career of Prince Charles, twenty-first Prince of Wales.

The engagement of His Royal Highness to Lady Diana Spencer has delighted the whole nation and Commonwealth. We now look forward to the first wedding in the direct line of succession to the Throne since 20 November 1947, when the Prince's parents, The Queen, then Princess Elizabeth, and Prince Philip, a serving Lieutenant, in the Royal Navy, married in Westminster Abbey. Any children which are born to Their Royal Highnesses The Prince and Princess of Wales will have the style of His or Her Royal Highness, and the titular dignity of Prince or Princess before their Christian names.

Most of the previous Princes of Wales chose their brides to fulfil

Lady Diana Spencer. From photographs taken during the harassing period before the engagement was announced.

Lady Diana Spencer and the Prince of Wales in the garden of Buckingham Palace after the announcement.

treaties of alliance or for other reasons of state. In many cases, they obeyed their father's command. For instance, George II selected Princess Augusta of Saxe-Gotha for his eldest son, Frederick, Prince of Wales, ordering him to 'take leave of a mistress whom he kept in so open a manner as he did Miss Vane.' Some of these marriages turned out quite well, while others, like the Prince Regent's, were quite disastrous.

Prince Charles has bided his time until well into his fourth decade, but those who knew his character were quite certain he would wait until he was in love, and that his bride would make an admirable Queen. Though most Princes have married when they were younger, there are precedents for older bridegrooms. King George IV was 32 when he married, the Black Prince was a year younger, and Frederick, Prince of Wales, was nearly 30.

The last occasion when a Prince of Wales married *as* Prince of Wales was well over a hundred years ago. In 1863, Prince Charles's great-great-grandfather, Prince Albert Edward, later King Edward VII, married the beautiful Princess Alexandra of Denmark, who happened to belong to the same family as Prince Philip.

It is sometimes forgotten that for almost half the time since the first Prince of Wales was created in 1301, there has been no Prince of Wales. Out of a total of nearly 680 years, there have been 374 years without a Prince of Wales. The longest period was 101 years, stretching from Henry VIII's accession in 1509 until the creation as Prince of Wales in 1610 of his great-great-great-nephew, Prince Henry, elder brother of Charles I. Strangely enough, Henry VIII, for all his joy at having a son and heir, never created the future Edward VI Prince of Wales, although there was some move to do so, when Henry's death intervened.

Prince Charles can trace his descent from six earlier Princes of Wales. There was the first Prince of Wales, the future Edward II, born in Caernarvon Castle, and brutally murdered in Berkeley Castle, three Hanoverian Princes, George II, his son, Prince Frederick, and his grandson, George III, and, in more recent years, Edward VII and George V.

It is worth noting that Lady Diana's background is very similar to that of the Queen Mother. Both are the daughters of Earls of ancient lineage and both have royal blood in their veins – Henry VII is a common ancestor. Lady Diana also descends from the same male line that produced Sir Winston Churchill. Both she and Prince Charles can also establish relationship with George Washington, first President of the United States of America.

Lady Diana, who looks every inch a Princess, with a strong character to match, will become the first Princess of Wales for over 70 years. The last was Queen Mary, who was Princess of Wales for only 8½ years before her husband succeeded to the throne as George V. In the popular imagination, though, the title was much more closely associated with the previous Princess of Wales, Princess Alexandra, wife of the future Edward VII, who held the title for almost 38 years of Queen Victoria's reign.

With so many recent members of her family with Royal Household appointments, Lady Diana is not unfamiliar to Court life and should not find it difficult to fulfil the exacting role of third lady in the land.

Prince Charles is the first Prince of Wales to live surrounded by the full glare of publicity. This does not seem to have affected him in any way, for he possesses a happy combination of informal approachability (his jokes are proverbial) with the same dedication to duty as the Queen and King George VI. We are indeed fortunate in our future King and Queen.

A Son
for the Princess

In November 1948 something so important happened that *The Times* went wild and placed a discreet announcement in the top right-hand corner of the front page, announcing 'A SON FOR THE PRINCESS'. No page reference was given, so fidgeting readers had no option but to purchase the paper in order to obtain further details regarding this dramatic news. Hidden in the middle of the paper was *The Court Circular,* to which all royalty watchers turn for the ultimate truth, presented without embellishment. It merely stated that 'The Princess Elizabeth, Duchess of Edinburgh, was safely delivered of a Prince at 9.14 p.m. today. Her Royal Highness and her son are both doing well.' Princess Elizabeth had not simply given birth to a baby boy, but to a Prince. *The Court Circular* acknowledged that this child was the one person in England whose life was predestined and who would have no free choice of career. One day this 7 lb 6 oz Prince would be King.

While the announcement was typed out and carefully checked, a lot of other things were happening. Queen Elizabeth embraced the Duke of Edinburgh, clad, according to his cousin, 'in unconventional shirt and flannels', after a game of squash and a swim, and the King shook him warmly by the hand. The Duke responded by opening a bottle of celebratory champagne. A servant crossed the forecourt of the Palace and tipped the wink to the Policeman at the gate who then relayed the news to the enormous crowd gathered at the railings and, as *The Times* reported, there was 'an outburst of excited comment.' Queen Mary, informed by telephone that she was now a great-grandmother, drove at

An outburst of excited comment. The crowd at Buckingham Palace in November 1948.

9

once from Marlborough House and was cheered enthusiastically by the crowd. Also cheered by the public was a man in the forecourt of the Palace, who was wrongly identified as the proud father. Amongst the loyal crowd was the Australian statesman Robert Menzies who, together with his family, had kept an excited vigil in the Mall throughout the day. 'The excitement was intense', wrote Sir Robert, 'We were all friends, and slapped the backs of perfect strangers with complete abandon.' Sir Robert was impressed by the 'democratic crowd', looking to the Crown as its focal point. Another telephone call went to Sandbach, home of the Earl of Scarbrough where Princess Margaret was staying. She was told that she was now an aunt – 'Charley's Aunt' as they called her – 'Probably my proudest title of all', she commented. A cable was sent to a sixty-three year old lady in a grey habit, engaged in charitable work on the island of Tinos, in the Aegean Sea. It arrived in the night and Princess Andrew of Greece learned that her most important grandson had been safely delivered. The birth of Prince Charles was significant because it meant that King George VI now had heirs in two generations. The succession was assured. It was the first birth in direct line of succession for over fifty years, and the first which had not taken place in the presence of a Minister of the Crown. Traditionally, the Home Secretary had to be in the vicinity to make sure that there was no swapping of infants. *The Times* leader hailed the birth as 'a national and imperial event which can for a moment divert the people's thoughts from the acrimonies of domestic argument and from the anxieties of the national scene.' *The Times* reminded its readers that through his father the young prince descended in the male line from the Danish Race 'which as the most recent historical studies all go to show is to be credited with a full half share in the ancestry of the English.' It was the first time that a royal prince had had Danish ancestry in the male line since King Harthacnut's death in 1042.

Prince Charles was fifth in descent from Queen Victoria, thirteenth from James I, thirty-second from William the Conqueror and thirty-ninth from Alfred the Great. Anglo-Saxon chronicles trace Alfred's pedigree back to the god Woden. Other distinguished and romantic progenitors of the young Prince included Charlemagne, St Louis, Frederick the Wonder of the World, Vortigern, Cadwallader, Neill of the Nine Hostages and the High Kings of Erin, and, stretching credulity to the limit, Musa ibn Naseir, an Arab Sheikh, born in Mecca in 660. On the maternal side Prince Charles counts George Smith, Mary Tucker and Frances Webb (also the progenitors of Fourth Man, Anthony Blunt) among his forbears. The prince is also fifth in descent from Anne Wellesley, the natural daughter of the Marquess Wellesley, brother of the 1st Duke of Wellington.

The birth of Prince Charles was greeted formally and enthusiastically in the House of Commons. Clement Attlee, the Prime Minister, commented on his future, saying:

'The young Prince may have to carry great responsibilities. He is the heir to a great tradition and we shall watch him growing to manhood with lively interest, knowing that in his own home he will receive a training, by example rather than mere precept, in that courtesy and in that gracious and tireless devotion to the manifold duties of constitutional monarchy which have won the hearts of our people.'

Then Mr Churchill rose to his feet and in a voice racked with deep emotion, greeted 'the little Prince, now born into this world of strife and storm'. He continued:

'I hope that amongst those principles that will be instilled into him will be the truth that the Sovereign is never so great as when the people are free. There we meet on common ground.'

So far no Keir Hardie had spoken, no warnings of the dangers of the future had been pronounced. But the Commons were slightly alarmed when Willie Gallacher rose to his feet. Gallacher was the Communist member for West Fife. In 1945 he had defeated the Labour candidate, one Lieutenant W. W. Hamilton, by just over 2,000 votes. He was destined to be the last Communist member in the House, because the Lieutenant ousted him in 1950. Willie Hamilton has held the seat ever since. However, the House need not have worried. Gallacher announced that he would make no adverse comment on the celebrations associated with the birth of 'this baby' because on the day of his own birth there had been 'bell ringing and joyful sounds in abundance'. This statement caused a good deal of amusement in the House which turned into loud laughter when the Communist member revealed that he had been born on a Christmas Sunday morning.

In the Lords, Viscount Hall saw it as a good omen that Prince Charles had come into the world on a Sunday. He quoted the well-known lines:

> ' a child that's born on Sabbath Day
> Is fair and wise and good and gay.'

Willie Gallacher, the Communist MP for West Fife. He rose to his feet.

The Marquess of Salisbury recognised the arrival of a new generation and described it as an event of transcending importance.

Meanwhile the news spread across England and to the furthest corners of the globe. The King's Troop, Royal Horse Artillery fired a salute of forty-one guns, the Navy spliced the mainbrace, Merioneth lit coast bonfires, Dolgelly decked its streets with flags and Prince William of Gloucester arrived at Buckingham Palace to meet his new cousin, carrying a small basket of roses. In Canada they sang the National Anthem, in Australia (ten years prematurely) they intoned 'God Bless the Prince of Wales'. New Zealand's telephone system was jammed in the middle of the morning by people ringing home with the news, Capetown put out bunting, India raised the National Flag on public buildings, and Kenya broadcast the glad tidings in seven native tongues. Ceylon rejoiced and Malta floodlit the buildings of Valetta. All in all Prince Charles's arrival on Sunday, 14 November did not pass unnoticed.

A new royal baby is likely to be observed with more avid attention than any other baby. Princess Elizabeth's governess, Marion Crawford saw him when he was four days old. She noted that like all the royal babies he bore a strong resemblance to King George V:

'this baby also had that absurdly mature look, and ridges under his eyes. He was very healthy and strong, and beautifully made, with a flawless, silky skin.'

Queen Mary, as much an expert on the provenance of royal physiognomy as on that of antiques and works of art, detected a likeness to the Prince Consort, and spent an entertaining afternoon with Lady Airlie, looking through old pictures of him. No photographs of Prince Charles were issued publicly for some time and a number of rumours spread that there was something wrong with the child. Madame Hélène Cordet unwittingly became involved in this drama. Prince Philip had told her mother, Madame Foufounis, that the baby was the picture of health and looked like a plum pudding. In an attempt to put an end to

The first official portraits of Prince Charles by Cecil Beaton. *Above:* with Princess Elizabeth. *Below:* alone.

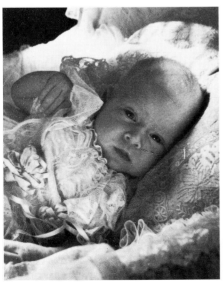

speculation in Paris, Mme Cordet quoted the remark and suddenly the Prince was nicknamed 'Plum Pudding' throughout France. Years later a French magazine investigated the origin of the sobriquet, and when Mme Cordet wrote to explain it, she received the reply: 'Among all the other legends we got about the origin of that nickname, yours is quite amusing, full of imagination and charming.' Soon, however, the Palace was to have far more serious matters to worry about. Just as Princess Elizabeth's birth had taken place during a traumatic period in the life of the nation – the General Strike of 1926 – so the joy at Prince Charles's birth soon gave way to anxiety about his grandfather's state of health.

On 23 November it was announced that King George VI was suffering from a serious vascular obstruction in his leg and had complained of a loss of feeling in his right foot. It was feared that his right leg might have to be amputated. His proposed tour of Australia and New Zealand was postponed indefinitely. The King rested in bed and remained under the close care of his doctors. The immediate danger passed and

by 15 December he was well enough to attend Prince Charles's christening in the Music Room of the Palace. Unlike his mother, who cried so much throughout her christening that a somewhat old-fashioned nurse administered a dose of dill water, Prince Charles behaved perfectly and took part in this ceremony, as in many to come, with appropriate dignity. The Archbishop of Canterbury, Dr Geoffrey Fisher, who had officiated at the wedding of Princess Elizabeth and the Duke of Edinburgh just over a year before, was able to maintain his genial boast that he had never had a casualty at a christening. The Archbishop baptized the Prince with the names 'Charles Philip Arthur George'. The choice of the name Charles was a break with modern tradition, the last reigning sovereign of that name being Charles II. Indeed, when the Prince's sister, born in 1950, was named Anne, it was believed that Princess Elizabeth was making a conscious attempt to revive royal Stuart names – a belief encouraged, no doubt, by the worthy editors of such publications as the *Royal Stuart Review*. But, in fact, the choice of these names had no special significance. The royal parents simply happened to like them best. The baby's second name, Philip, was inherited from his father, of course, and the last two names from his grandfather.

His eight godparents were interesting choices, all closely related to the Prince. Besides his grandparents, the King and Queen and his aunt, Princess Margaret, they included King Haakon of Norway, who had spent some time in London during the war and had married King George V's sister, Princess Maud, and the Hon. David Bowes-Lyon, the favourite brother of Queen Elizabeth. The other three were relations of the Duke of Edinburgh. Prince Philip's grandmother, the eighty-five year old Dowager Marchioness of Milford Haven, came from Kensington Palace. She belonged to that august family gerontocracy, the granddaughters of Queen Victoria, and though she only had two years left in which to perform the duties of a godparent, she could take pride in being the progenitor not only of the Mountbattens but of a future King. The Marchioness's granddaughter, Lady Brabourne, was another godmother. She was the daughter of Earl Mountbatten of Burma, under whose supervision Prince Philip had

Three generations hold Prince Charles after his christening. From left to right: Queen Mary; Queen Elizabeth (now the Queen Mother); and Princess Elizabeth (now The Queen).

The first picture of the family together— Princess Elizabeth, the Duke of Edinburgh and Prince Charles.

Prince George of Greece, one of the Prince's godfathers.

been educated. In 1979, she succeeded to her father's title and is now known as Countess Mountbatten of Burma. The last god-parent was the magnificent Prince George of Greece, the only surviving brother of Prince Philip's father. Prince George's career was a fascinating one. In his youth he had been a close friend of Nicholas, the last Tsar of Russia, and had toured Japan with him. In a small town, called Otso, a Japanese policeman, who was running beside the Tsarevitch's rickshaw, suddenly turned on him and slashed him over the head with his sword. Prince George was quick to react, and swiftly felled the assailant with a blow from a heavy bamboo cane. Evidently, the man was a Samurai, who had taken a vow to rid Japan of all foreigners. Later Prince George became High Commissioner for the Powers in Crete, but fell victim to the propaganda of Venizelos and had to resign. He married Princess Marie Bonaparte, who became a celebrated philosopher and historian and the *belle amie* of Aristide Briand. Prince George, who died in 1957, aged eighty-eight, embodied many of the finer characteristics of a godfather, though he seems to have met Prince Charles only at the Coronation. He had been very fond of the Duke of Edinburgh as a boy, and when times were hard, had dipped into his wife's fortune to help the Duke's parents.

As is traditional on the occasion of a royal event, the Poet Laureate set to work to earn his £27 a year.

> *A Hope for the Newly Born*
> May destiny, allotting what befalls,
> Grant to the newly-born this saving grace
> A guard more sure than ships and fortress-walls,
> The loyal love and service of a race.
>
> John Masefield

Again the Christening attracted huge crowds. Harold Nicolson suggested in his diary the reason for this enthusiasm: 'It is the identification of natural human experience with this strange royal world that causes these emotions; one's own life enlarged into a fairy story.'

When Prince Charles was six months old, his mother gave him a teddy bear and his father a tiny cricket bat, more for ceremonial use than play, one suspects. In July 1949 the Edinburghs moved to Clarence House and the Prince went with them. There were pram-rides at Windlesham Manor, Surrey, and occasional photographs of the Prince driving out with Nurse Lightbody. Otherwise his early years were uneventful. He gave great pleasure to his dynastically conscious great-grandmother Queen Mary at Marlborough House. He called her Gan-Gan and retains a vivid impression of her, sitting very upright, her feet on a footstool, surrounded by her famous collection of jade. Age had mellowed the old Queen's severity, for whereas the Queen and Princess Margaret were never allowed to touch the objects when they were little, she let him play with anything he liked. Queen Mary was delighted to be a great-grandmother. Her christening gift to the Prince was a silver gilt cup and cover which had originally been given by George III to one of his godsons in 1780. And Queen Mary herself noted: 'I gave a present from my great grandfather, to my great grandson 168 years later'. The Prince also remembers King George VI. Still clear in his memory is a photographic session on his third birthday. The King, 'somebody much bigger', sat beside the Prince while another figure (who later turned out to be the Press Secretary, Richard Colville) swung 'something shiny on the end of his watch chain' in an attempt to capture the boy's attention. In years clouded by illness and anxiety, King George VI enjoyed the company of his eventual heir, and wrote to his daughter:

'He is too sweet stumping around the room, we shall love having him at Sandringham. He is the fifth generation to live there and I hope he will get to love the place.'

One of the advantages of being predestined to reign is that from the earliest days, Prince Charles has been able to meet the great statesmen of former days and glean from them and others tales unlikely to be imparted to anyone else of his age. While he was growing up he spent a considerable amount of time with Sir Winston Churchill. An early impression of him was of 'a large man, a large hat and a huge cigar.' He also met and struck up a friendship with Eisenhower. When the General came to stay, he inscribed a number of lapel badges with the words 'I like Ike' and persuaded a number of footmen to emulate his

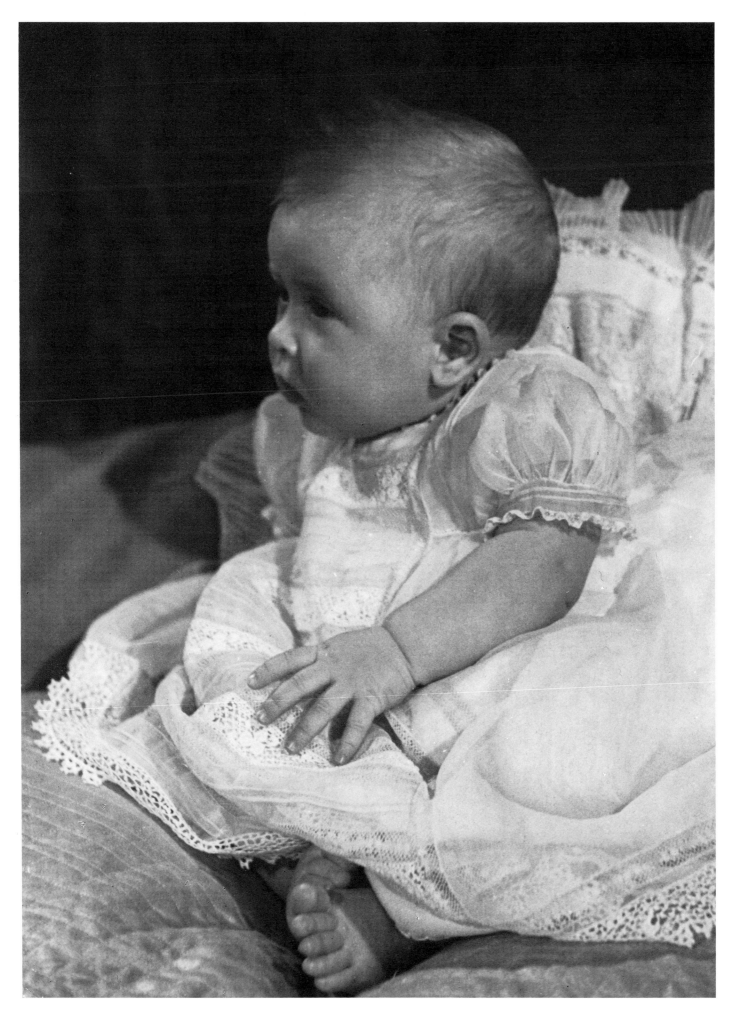

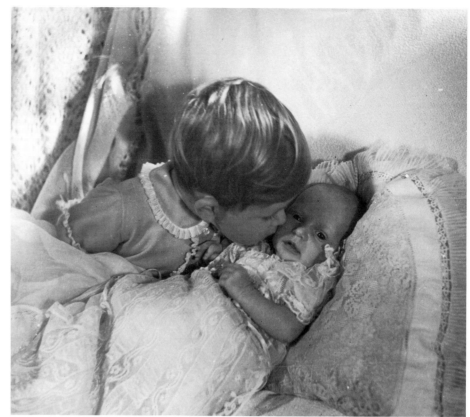

Above, left and right: early pictures of Prince Charles and his new sister, Princess Anne.

Left: Prince Charles watching The King's Birthday Parade. *Below:* Prince Charles with his mother at Ballater, Scotland.

Right: The Christening of Princess Anne in 1950. *Standing*—King George VI and the Duke of Edinburgh. *Seated*—Queen Mary, Princess Elizabeth with Princess Anne, Prince Charles with Queen Elizabeth.

Prince Charles waving with his mother at the age of two.

Left:
An outing in Green Park on Prince Charles's second birthday, November 1950.

Right:
The royal children with their parents in the grounds of Clarence House in August 1951.

example by wearing them. He always enjoyed listening to the reminiscences of Princess Alice, Countess of Athlone and hearing his grandmother, Princess Andrew of Greece bring Queen Victoria to life for him with her wealth of vivid, personal impressions. Queen Victoria Eugénie of Spain also used to tell him 'fascinating stories about life at Windsor towards the end of the last century.'

Meanwhile, the Duke of Edinburgh continued active service in Malta, where he had been posted in October 1949. Princess Elizabeth joined him when time and official duties permitted, and Prince Charles spent Christmas with his grandparents. Princess Anne was born at Clarence House on 15 August 1950.

All too soon the reign of King George VI came to an end. Lord Chandos, then Oliver Lyttelton and Secretary of State for the Colonies remembers being present at London Airport, as the King waved goodbye to Princess Elizabeth and the Duke of Edinburgh on the first leg of a tour of East Africa, Australia and New Zealand.

'I was shocked by the King's appearance. I was familiar with his look and mien, but he seemed much altered and strained. I had the feeling of doom . . . I felt with deep foreboding that this would be the last time he was to see his daughter, and that he thought so himself.'

Right: Prince Charles with Queen Elizabeth waiting to greet Princess Elizabeth and the Duke of Edinburgh on their return from Canada (17 November 1951).

Far right: Prince Charles and Princess Anne with their grandparents, The King and Queen at Buckingham Palace on Prince Charles's third birthday in 1951. This was the first photograph of the King since his serious illness.

Prince Charles and Princess Anne arriving at Ballater Station, nine miles from Balmoral, on their way home from their Scottish holiday in 1953.

A week later, on 6 February, Princess Elizabeth 'became Queen while perched in a tree in Africa' and Prince Charles automatically became Duke of Cornwall and Rothesay, Earl of Carrick and Baron of Renfrew, Lord of the Isles and Great Steward of Scotland, and, more simply, Heir to the Throne. He did not become Prince of Wales for another six years. It meant a lot of changes, but the Queen decided that Prince Charles and Princess Anne need not go through the ritual of bowing and curtseying to her as their Sovereign as well as their mother, though out of deference to Queen Mary, they did so when at Marlborough House.

One of the early constitutional problems that arose was the delicate question of the name of the Royal House. A Queen Regnant is the last of her line, and her son inherits his father's name and founds a new house. Though British Royal Highnesses sign everything with their Christian names only, there was no doubt that, in common law, Prince Charles and Princess Anne bore the surname of Mountbatten. Neither King George VI nor Winston Churchill had been very happy about this. King George VI had declared in letters patent three days before Prince Charles's birth that he was to have the style of Royal Highness and be called Prince ———; otherwise he would simply have been born a Mountbatten though he would have adopted one of his father's titles as a courtesy title. For example he might have been known as the Earl of Merioneth. Royal children get no title from their mother (unless she is the Sovereign) as was shown in the case of Princess Margaret's children, and Princess Anne's son, who was born in 1977 as Master Peter Phillips. There was nothing wrong with the name Mountbatten. Indeed at the Prince's birth *The Times* commented:

'Some day he may inaugurate a dynasty bearing the name of Mountbatten, which in the last half-century has been surpassed by none in its record of public service.'

It is worth investigating how it was that the Duke of Edinburgh became a Mountbatten. Originally he was a member of the Greek Royal House, which is Danish in origin. Not a drop of Greek blood flows through his veins. He belonged to the House of Schleswig-Holstein-Sonderburg-Glucksburg. Anxious to become a British citizen, and to serve in the British Navy, Prince Philip let it be known that he would like to become 'Lieutenant Philip ——— R.N.' Possible names were suggested, for example Oldcastle, an anglicized version of Oldenburg, dreamed up by

A portrait of Prince Charles by Stella Marks.

Prince Charles and Princess Anne watching the Changing of the Guard at Windsor Castle in April 1953. The Queen Mother can be seen in the centre window.

the heralds, but rejected as unsuitable. Finally, Prince Philip became a Mountbatten, the name which had been adopted by his maternal grandfather, Prince Louis of Battenberg, when he renounced his foreign titles on 14 July 1917. The surname of Mountbatten was never used by Prince Philip's mother, because she had married Prince Andrew of Greece, fourteen years before 1917. Prince Philip had not been so keen on the name, because it identified him too closely with his distinguished uncle, but he admitted later: 'I couldn't think of a reasonable alternative.' It is therefore not at all surprising that at the dawn of the new reign Churchill suggested that the Queen should take official steps to preserve the dynastic name of Windsor. On 9 April 1952 the *London Gazette* announced:

'The Queen today declared in Council Her Will and Pleasure that She and Her Children shall be styled and known as the House and Family of Windsor, and that Her descendants, other than female descendants who marry, and their descendants shall bear the name of Windsor.'

On 8 February 1960 a further declaration was made to the effect that the family would in future generations be called Mountbatten-Windsor. It was never made absolutely clear whether or not this made Prince Charles a Mountbatten-Windsor but it now seems certain to have done so. Princess Anne's name on the marriage register was given

23

as 'Anne Elizabeth Alice Louise Mountbatten-Windsor', though she still signed herself 'Anne'. The form in which Prince Charles's name appears on the register will be eagerly examined. If he is similarly described, he will found the new House of Mountbatten-Windsor. However, the Central Office of Information stated, as recently as 1972:

'In 1952 Queen Elizabeth decreed that she and her children should be known as the House and Family of Windsor. Prince Charles retains the name despite the Queen's decision in February 1960 to make different provision for the name of certain of her descendants.'

Harold Macmillan was one of the members of the Cabinet who agreed to the Lord Chancellor's proposals concerning the name of the Royal House. In his memoirs he gives the impression that he certainly regarded Windsor as the proper name for Prince Charles:

'. . . the "name" of the House, Family and Dynasty to be Windsor – the name of any 'de-royalised' grandson, etc. of the Queen and Prince Philip to be 'Mountbatten-Windsor' like Spencer-Churchill.'

Constitutional lawyers and genealogists, however, maintain that Prince Charles belongs to the House and Family of Windsor but that his surname is Mountbatten-Windsor.

Prince Charles was still living in what Violet Bonham-Carter called 'the dazzling dusk of infancy' and was therefore too young to attend King George VI's funeral – he stayed at Sandringham. He was also too

Prince Charles and his first horn.

The Royal Family by Karsh of Ottawa in the summer of 1951.

24

The royal children in a train at Aberdeen in August 1952.
Below: on their way to the Birthday Parade with the Queen Mother and Princess Margaret on 11 June 1953.

young to sit through the lengthy Coronation, but the four year old boy watched the crowds growing outside the Palace and is said to have found the scene most exciting. He ran from the window to the Queen Mother to report on the events of that wet but wonderful day which he watched in dazed astonishment. He was saved the alarming experience of his third cousin, once removed, King Michael of Roumania, who at the age of five had been placed on a throne to be officially recognised by the National Assembly. On that occasion the boy King sat on a throne, his feet not even touching the ground, while his mother, Princess Helen stood beside him, pale under her black veil. At the end of the ceremony she led him to the side of the dais, and he made a brave little salute. Suddenly the adults around him seemed to go mad crying out 'Hurrah! Hurrah! Hurrah! Long live King Michael!' It was too much for the boy, who in the midst of this hysteria buried his head in the folds of his mother's dress. Reassured by this tender presence, the frightened young King regained his composure and once again saluted the delirious assembly.

The Sovereign's heir is normally the first peer to do obeisance at the throne, but rightly it was thought that the Prince might be overcome by even attending the lengthy services, the quaint processes of the ceremony, the music, the shouting and the emotion. However, it would have been a crime to deny him the experience of seeing his mother crowned, and accordingly he was driven from the Palace to a side-door of Westminster Abbey, where he arrived in his white silk suit, his hair shining with brilliantine. He entered the Abbey, between Mrs Lightbody and a Coldstream Guards officer. He took his place in the royal

box between his grandmother and Princess Margaret, just as the Queen prepared to be anointed. Apart from a certain amount of exploring in the royal box, the Prince comported himself well and saw St Edward's Crown being placed on his mother's head. Later in the day he and Princess Anne joined the Royal Family on the balcony. The Prince was wearing his first decoration, the Queen's Coronation medal, one he still wears every time he puts on full-dress uniform. For the 1953 Birthday Parade the young Prince had learned to make a fine salute although the gesture seemed to puzzle his great-aunt, the Princess Royal.

Coronation Day scenes at Buckingham Palace on 2 June 1953.

Prince Charles and Princess Anne in their Coronation Day clothes.

Above: Prince Charles with his great-aunt, Lady Mountbatten, in Malta in April 1954.

Below: On board *Britannia* at Gibraltar in May 1954.

Right: Prince Charles arriving at Custom House Quay, Valetta in May 1954. Waiting to greet him is the Governor of Malta, Sir Gerald Creasy.

Prince Charles and Princess Anne in the garden at Royal Lodge, Windsor in April 1954.

Prince Charles began his education at the Palace with a governess, Katherine Peebles, formerly governess to Prince Michael of Kent and affectionately known as 'Miss P.'. This was a break with tradition as royal tutors were normally male. As he grew up the Prince enjoyed reading and geography, found history interesting, but was stumped by mathematics. He made educational visits to Madame Tussaud's and the Planetarium. The Duke of Edinburgh gave him his first swimming lesson – Prince Charles could swim by the age of six – and took him on his first speedboat ride. They went coot-shooting together on the Norfolk broads and sailing in fairly rough weather, all this at an age when most upper class boys were still in the charge of their nannies. The Duke put him on his first pony and he later took riding lessons on a Welsh mountain pony. He was very frightened when he started riding, and his present day confidence in the saddle at the Birthday Parade and when hunting has been achieved only after a long struggle with his nerves.

How did the Palace staff see him at this time? They agree that he was 'an exceptionally sweet natured little boy' and speak of his 'thoughtfulness' towards others. He was developing 'a bubbling sense of humour' but tended to be rather shy. Unlike other members of the Royal Family, when young, he took no pleasure in having the sentries salute him.

Schooldays were interrupted when Prince Charles and Princess Anne boarded the Royal Yacht Britannia in 1954 to join the Queen and the Duke of Edinburgh on the last leg of their Commonwealth Tour. Seen off by the Queen Mother and Princess Margaret, Prince Charles shook hands with Rear-Admiral A. G. V. Hubbach at Portsmouth Dockyard, showing the composure of a budding public relations officer. It was the maiden voyage of Britannia and the Prince took a lively interest in all that went on. In Tobruk, Prince Charles swopped his Hayfords overcoat for a sailor suit. In Malta the two royal children enjoyed exploring the rocks and coves with their great-aunt, Lady

Prince Charles and his sister dressed in popular current trends. *Above:* Meeting a Gibraltar ape. *Below:* About to leave for Balmoral after the Gibraltar visit.

Mountbatten. In fact soon after this trip Prince Charles's sense of style was recognised by *The Tailor and Cutter* – though the accolade was not entirely earned since the Prince had little say in his choice of clothing at the time. 'That austerely professional journal' as Dermot Morrah described it 'which judges mankind as so many animated dummies for the display of the masterpieces of the craft,' placed Prince Charles first in a list of eleven best-dressed men of the year. The following citation was made:

'His Baby-Bow and Fawn Stalker, followed by his junior fashion for a double-breasted woolly, is accentuated this year by his adoption of a very popular style among older folk. His velvet-collared topcoat also follows a popular current trend.'

In London in February 1955 Prince Charles and his sister were put on show after a lunch party the Queen was giving for the Shah of Persia and Queen Soraya. Sir Winston and Lady Churchill were there, and so was Harold Nicolson, King George V's biographer. The latter scrutinized the progeny of the old King and noted:

'The children then came in and are very well-behaved and natural. Prince Charles crams his mouth with coffee-sugar; Princess Anne picks at it delicately.'

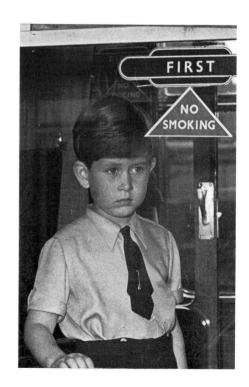

A kilted Prince Charles escorting Princess Anne in the grounds of Abergeldie Castle, Deeside, in August 1955.

Throughout their childhood both Prince Charles and Princess Anne received a fair amount of unpopular press. Prince Charles was described in 1955 as a forlorn little fellow, who had never been to the seaside. As it happened, he had been building sandcastles on the beach at Brancaster with Prince Philip only a fortnight before. Reports such as these were more galling to his parents, of course, than to the Prince. The press even made unkind remarks about his physical appearance. Expressions such as 'this jug-eared boy' serve as a reminder of his lack of popularity at that time. It was not really until Prince Charles made his first broadcast in 1969 that the general public had a chance to be charmed by his endearing personality.

A Tough Education

One of the most difficult problems that confronted the Queen and the Duke of Edinburgh was a suitable education for their son and heir. Edward VII's education, arranged by Prince Albert, had been placed in the hands of a string of private tutors, many of whom advocated strong physical discipline and all of whom recommended less bookwork. One French tutor even wrote: 'Make him climb trees! Run! Leap! Row! Ride! In many ways savages are much better educated than we are.' His advice was ignored. Later the Prince undertook a highly organized educational trip to Rome and somewhat interrupted stints at three universities, Edinburgh, Oxford and Cambridge. The most successful part of his education was a lengthy trip to Canada and the United States. One of his biographers reached the following conclusion on his upbringing:

'He was educated upon pedantic and rigid lines, which made his boyhood a weariness and his adolescence a struggle for emancipation.'

Edward VII's second son, the future King George V, did not become the heir to his father and grandmother until he was twenty-seven. This was generally considered to be a disadvantage, but may not have been.

Princess Anne and Prince Charles. A portrait study by Snowdon.

Antony Armstrong-Jones's portrait study of the Royal Family in the garden of Buckingham Palace. The composition was originally intended to show the royal children fishing, and Antony Armstrong-Jones accordingly hired a rod and caught two trout. Unfortunately, his housekeeper cooked the fish for his breakfast so the royal children were shown reading a book instead.

Prince Charles aged seven in the grounds of Balmoral.

Both King George V and his second son, King George VI were admirable monarchs, although neither had been born Heir to the Throne. As a result they had a somewhat easier youth with fewer pressures, unlike King Edward VIII, who finally found the burden too great for him. Prince Charles was brought up as a future King, and gradually became aware of what the future held in store for him. In 1969 he told Jack de Manio:

'I think it's something that dawns on you with the most ghastly, inexorable sense. I didn't wake up in my pram one day and say "Yippee, I . . ." you know. But I think it just dawns on you, you know, slowly that people are interested in one and slowly you get the idea that you have a certain duty and responsibility . . .'

King George V entered the Navy when he was thirteen and joined the Britannia at Dartmouth. He travelled round the world, accompanied by his tutor, the Rev. J. N. Dalton (father of Hugh Dalton), and subsequently passed his exam as sub-Lieutenant for the Royal Naval College at Greenwich, obtaining a first class in seamanship. He was later described by Admiral Hay as 'an accomplished naval officer, no carpet seaman, but one who has served like the rest of us.' His naval career was curtailed by his brother's death in 1892. It was no doubt his love of the sea that caused King George V to make his now famous remark: 'My brother and I never went to a preparatory school. The navy will teach David all he needs to know.' John Gore, King George V's biographer, told us that the King 'was well aware that his education as a sailor had ill fitted him for many of his new responsibilities.' It took Sir Arthur Bigge's influence during the years of King Edward VII's reign to 'repair the gaps in his knowledge of English and Constitutional History and to attain the normal education standard of the average public-schoolboy at the leaving age.' It is, therefore, astonishing that the King should have put such faith in the Navy. The Duke of Windsor has left a grim account of his early years at Osborne and Dartmouth. He then went to Magdalen College, Oxford, where he enjoyed the opportunities for sport and integrated well with the other undergraduates. 'All the time', his tutor wrote, 'he was learning more every day of men, gauging character, watching its play, getting to know what Englishmen are like, both individually and still more in the mass.' King George VI was nineteen when World War I broke out. Like his brother, he had been educated at Osborne and Dartmouth, but unlike him he remained there and served on board H.M.S. Collingwood in the Battle of Jutland in 1916. Despite ill health, he did well in the Navy and later joined the Royal Navy Air Force (which amalgamated with the Royal Flying Corps in 1918 and became the R.A.F.). With his brother, Prince Henry, later Duke of Gloucester, he spent some terms at Trinity College, Cambridge. 'Their freshness and willingness to learn made for a very pleasant relationship between tutor and pupil' we are told, 'and all who came in contact with them . . . were delighted with their naturalness and friendliness.'

The present Queen's education was one of the focal points of the two famous attacks on the monarchy by John Grigg and Malcolm Muggeridge in 1957. Grigg remarked: 'Crawfie, Sir Henry Marten, the London season, the racecourse, the grouse moor, Canasta and the occasional royal tour – all this would not have been good enough for Queen Elizabeth I!' And he was worried about Prince Charles's future:

'. . . will (the Queen) have the wisdom to give her children an education very different from her own? Will she, above all, see to it that Prince Charles is equipped with all the knowledge he can absorb without injury to his health, and that he mixes during his formative years . . . not merely with future landowners or stockbrokers?'

For this and other attacks John Grigg, or Lord Altrincham as he then was, became the victim of one of Britain's periodic outbursts of national hysteria. Two thousand letters arrived at his house within the first week. He was anathematized by the Archbishop of Canterbury menaced with all sorts of hideous deaths by various staunch monarchists, slapped across the face by a member of the League of Empire Loyalists, threatened with expulsion from his club and challenged to a duel. Enough dung was tipped through his letter-box to manure his window-boxes for the season, and it was even rumoured that his name was to be struck from the Old Etonian List of Members (though Grigg reckoned that he was saved from that fate by the high cost of reprinting it).

Prince Charles and his sister enjoying country life. *Above:* at a meeting of the West Norfolk Foxhounds in January 1957. *Below:* at Badminton in 1960.

Prince Charles coming out of Hill House with his Headmaster after his first day at school. Buckingham Palace requested that the name and number be obliterated from the picture before publication.

The Queen chatting to Prince Philip during a polo match at Smith's Lawn, while the royal children and the corgi look on.

Palace reaction to Grigg's outcry was mixed, but the Duke of Edinburgh certainly took it to heart. The planning of Prince Charles's education received very serious thought. He was likely to become King at the end of the twentieth century and in a fast changing world serious consideration had to be given to the type of training which would equip him best for his task.

Prince Charles left the Palace nursery on 7 November 1956 and spent nine months at Hill House, a pre-preparatory school in Hans Place, Knightsbridge. His first few weeks there consisted of afternoon visits, a gradual process of acquainting himself with the school, his class-mates and the afternoon games. It had been hoped that Prince Charles would be able to attend the school without a blaze of publicity. But news is news and cameramen have a job to do and the arrival at school of the first Heir to the Throne ever to attend a day school was of prime interest to readers. The photographers flashed away and pictures of the small figure in his conker coloured cap circumnavigated the globe. The press respected his privacy only to the extent of not naming the school.

Residents and shoppers in S.W.1 are well accustomed to the crocodiles of Hill House boys who file through Knightsbridge, doffing their caps ceremoniously to motorists who pause at pedestrian crossings. In Prince Charles's day, the young men were made of sterner stuff than today's brood. Shorts were the order of the day whatever the weather and those warm looking corduroy plus-fours were a thing of the future. Whereas Prince Charles was nearly eight when he started at the school, most boys attended from the age of four to eight and were then despatched to some South of England preparatory school. It was the first leg on a journey through public school to university. The quality of teaching was good – little boys could put in a year or more of Latin and French, and have a good start on their contemporaries at boarding school later on. The school was well-equipped with a myriad of rooms, linoleum covered stairs, up and down which tiny feet made an inordinate noise between school classes, a gymnasium, which some enjoyed and others detested, a stage for smaller theatricals, and a dining-room where rather unexceptional food was served – a rude awakening to the reality of institutional meals.

The school was run by Colonel and Mrs. Townend. The Colonel, dubbed with the sobriquet 'Sir' to the extent of its appearance in such phrases as: 'Sir says you've got to stop doing that', was a believer in discipline and good behaviour, the first principle of which was 'leadership from the front by example.' There was no corporal punishment, but the Colonel had a certain presence which commanded respect. His wife helped him to run the school and took a lot of trouble to explain to the young boys not only what they were aiming to achieve, but how and why.

Prince Charles's first school report reveals that he loved history, had made 'a fair start' at latin, read very well, and had 'a sweet voice, especially in lower register' when he sang. Arithmetic remained a problem. Another part of Prince Charles's general education was advanced. He paid his first visit to a shop, he learned to handle money for the first time and he took his first journey on a London bus, a voyage he hugely enjoyed.

Prince Charles left Hill House in the summer of 1957. He was described as a slow developer, though he had a retentive memory and 'a little above average intelligence.' The Queen had to make a serious decision as to where Prince Charles should now go. A number of possible places were inspected under the guise of a royal visit, and each in turn was then given star-billing in the newspaper as the most likely

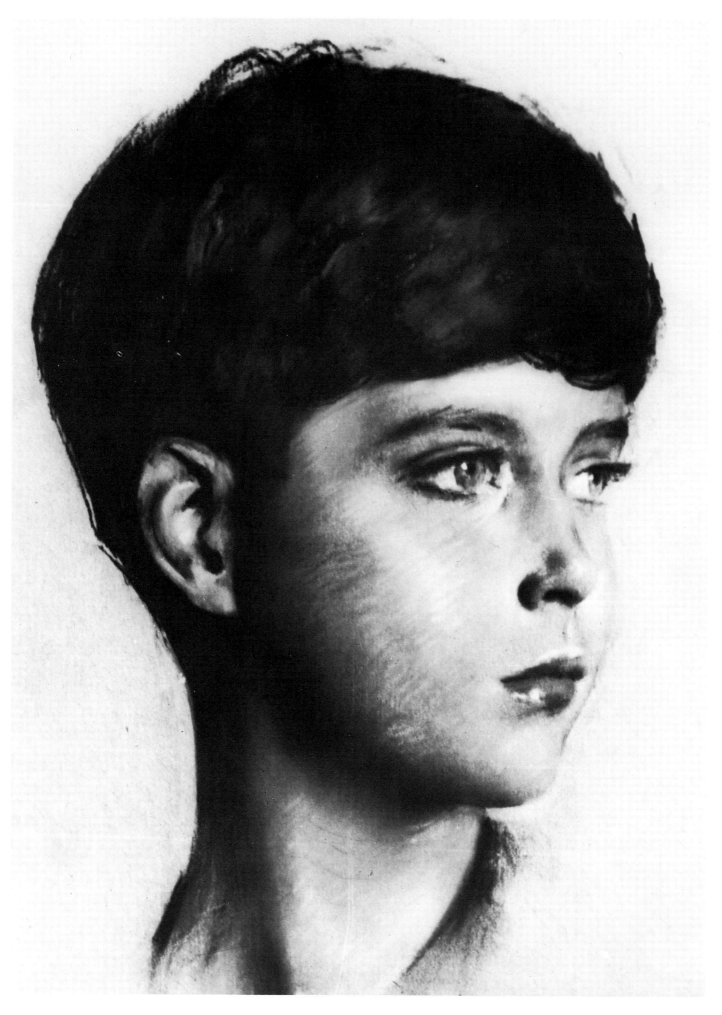

Prince Charles. A study by A. K. Lawrence, RA, RP, shown at the Royal Society of Portrait Painters Exhibition in November 1957.

School Sports Day.

school for the Prince. In the end, however, the Prince slipped firmly into his father's footprints and followed him to Cheam, a preparatory school at Headley on the Berkshire Downs. The Duke of Edinburgh had gone there when he was nine and he enjoyed it, though he did not excel. Always ready to play down his own academic achievements, the Duke told old boys once 'I belonged to the batch of Cheam boys who were just sufficiently educated to be snapped up by the Services in the war.'

Cheam was certainly the most trying period of Prince Charles's life. He had not the slightest wish to leave home, being devoted to his family. He said later:

'I've never wanted *not* to have a home life – to get away from home. I love my home life. We happen to be a very close-knit family. I'm happier at home, with the family, than anywhere else.'

He gives the happiness of his home life as the reason he did not enjoy school as much as he might have done. Leaving Balmoral for Cheam was misery for him. Like Queen Victoria, he had grown very fond of the Scottish castle. On reading her journals when he was a litle older, he immediately sympathized with her first impressions of it, 'All seemed to breathe freedom and peace, and to make one forget the world and its sad turmoils.' 'She hated leaving', said Prince Charles, 'much as I hate leaving this marvellous place.'

Prince Charles and schoolfriends walking back to Cheam from church the day after he was created Prince of Wales, 27 July 1958.

Both the Queen and the Duke of Edinburgh accompanied Prince Charles on the long journey to Cheam. A few hours after his arrival at the school he was found 'standing apart, very much alone and very miserable.' His fellow pupils just did not know how to treat him, so they avoided him. Another problem was the press coverage of his activities. Prince Charles had a detective to ensure, amongst other things, that he was not the victim of photographers; nevertheless out of the eighty-eight days of his first term, there were only twenty on which some fanciful story connected with his way of life did not appear in a national newspaper. Finally the Press Office at Buckingham Palace had to summon the editors for a conference after which life became a bit easier. One item concerned the Prince being a victim of the major flu epidemic which swept Great Britain. His doctor, harrassed by journalists, was moved to comment: 'I have patients in hospital and a busy practice. Enquiries about Prince Charles are not helping me.'

An important event occurred on 26 July 1958. This was the day on which the Queen announced that her son had been created Prince of Wales. Until 1958 he was officially known as the Duke of Cornwall, a title to which the eldest son of the Sovereign succeeds automatically in accordance with the charter of 17 March 1337. The title of Prince of Wales has to be conferred by letters patent. Prince Charles is the twenty-first Prince of Wales, the first one being Edward, son of Edward I, who became Edward II in July 1307. The title is held until the Prince becomes King and then merges again with the Crown. Unlike most

Prince Charles steps away from a Welsh collie as the Royal Family arrive in Holyhead. This was his first visit to Welsh soil since he received his title of Prince of Wales. August 1958.

other titles it is not inherited by an heir if the Prince of Wales dies. The title dies with him and has to be recreated. The future George III, for example, was created Prince of Wales three weeks after the death of his father, Prince Frederick, during the lifetime of George II. On becoming Prince of Wales, Prince Charles also became Earl of Chester, as the two titles have been inseparably linked by statute since 1398. As if this was not enough, he also became a Knight of the Garter. Since the foundation of the Order in 1348, the Prince of Wales has always been a member. This did not mean that Prince Charles, then aged nine years and eight months, suddenly took possession of a coronet and a garter. The two investitures were delayed until his education was completed. They need not have been, but it was obviously more sensible that they were.

The Queen had hoped to make the announcement herself when she opened the Commonwealth Games at Cardiff but she fell victim to sinus trouble and had to have an operation. The Duke of Edinburgh went instead and when the games were over, he introduced a recorded message from the Queen, which was broadcast across the stadium. The Queen said:

'The British Empire and Commonwealth Games in the Capital together with all the activities of the Festival of Wales, have made this a memorable year for the Principality. I have therefore decided to mark it further by an act which will, I hope, give as much pleasure to all

The Prince of Wales waiting with his mother to greet the Duke of Edinburgh on his return from a 36,000 mile world tour in April 1959.

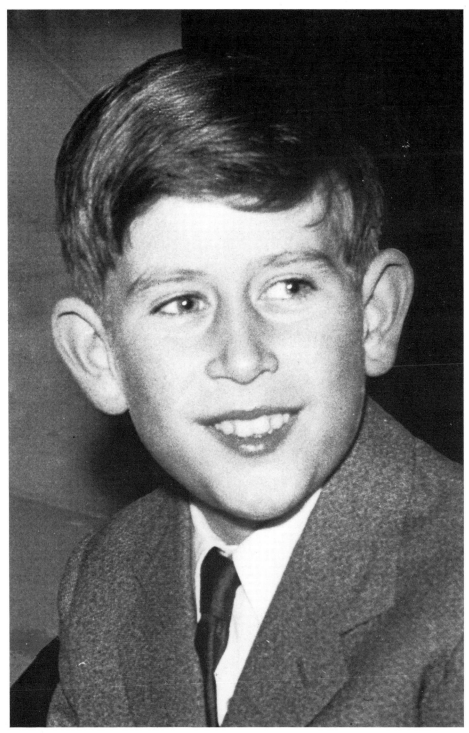

Prince Charles in 1959.

Welshmen as it does to me. I intend to create my son Charles, Prince of Wales today.'

The crowd responded by singing 'God Bless The Prince of Wales' with great gusto. The Queen's voice, mechanically controlled until the singing had died down, then continued:

'When he is grown up I will present him to you at Caernarvon.'

The Headmaster of Cheam, Peter Beck, knew about the announcement and invited Prince Charles and a few of his friends to his study to watch the ceremony on television. Prince Charles recalled later:

'I remember being acutely embarrassed when it was announced. I heard this marvellous great cheer coming from the stadium and for a little boy of nine it was rather bewildering.'

Prince Charles taking a look at Prince Andrew at Buckingham Palace in 1969. The photograph was taken by Cecil Beaton.

Having the Prince of Wales on the premises of the school meant that some special precautions had to be taken. In November 1959 additional police were seen lurking in the school grounds. Their presence was explained as a precaution against spontaneous eleventh birthday photographs, but is believed in fact to have been the result of a warning of a possible attempt by Irish extremists to kidnap the Prince and hold him as a hostage in order to bring about the end of Partition. The IRA denied any such attempt, but the police kept a close eye on the activities of a bunch of breakaway gunmen, called Fianna Uladh (The Warriors of Ulster). The Prince's eagle-eyed detective raised the alarm one night when he spotted a dark figure exploring the roof. A thorough search was made and sleeping heads were counted in the dormitories, but nothing unusual was discovered. Much later the mystery was solved. The figure had been a boy called Daukes, clad in pyjamas, who had narrowly escaped 'six of the best' by regaining the sanctity of his bed in the nick of time. In February of the following year Prince Charles acquired a brother, Prince Andrew. He was delighted with the news. Prince Andrew arrived during a crucial week for the Royal Family. Within seven days, the Marquess of Carisbrooke and Countess Mountbatten of Burma died, Prince Andrew was born and Princess Margaret announced her engagement to Antony Armstrong-Jones.

Prince Charles and Princess Anne pulling their young brother's pram at Balmoral in 1960.

Prince Charles rose in the hierarchy of Cheam to be the Captain of the Soccer XI, despite the fact that he hated team games – the only one he now plays is polo – and to be a School Monitor. He played the somewhat inappropriate role of Richard III in *The Last Baron*, a performance which was examined by the dramatic critic of the *Cheam School Chronicle:*

'Prince Charles played the traditional Gloucester with competence and depth: he had a good voice and excellent elocution, and very well conveyed the ambition and bitterness of the twisted hunchback.'

He also sang in the school choir. He left the school in July 1962 and in a final school report was judged to be good but not priggish, considerate to others, open-hearted and incapable of malice. Scholastically he was a conscientious all-rounder, although mathematics was still his weak point.

Corporal punishment seems to have been applied twice, a decision which was later to prove something of an embarrassment to Prince

Prince Charles on his way to the wedding of The Duke of Kent to Miss Katharine Worsley in Yorkshire in June 1961.

Charles's headmaster. During a visit to Tasmania in October 1974, the Prince of Wales met Peter Beck's son, Philip. The Prince said: 'I remember your father well. He caned me once – no twice.' The punishment was for ragging. Poor Mr. Beck, who had retired in 1963, was tracked down by the press to the fishing village of Tarbert in Argyllshire. The headmaster's comment was suitably discreet:

'I am not prepared to say anything about what happened except to say that the memory of Prince Charles will be much better than mine.'

Left: The Queen and Prince Charles at Badminton Horse Trials in 1961.

Below: The Queen, the Duke of Edinburgh and Prince Charles on the occasion of the wedding of The Duke of Kent to Miss Katharine Worsley.

Prince Charles photographed by Lord Snowdon.

The Queen Mother with her first three grandchildren in 1960.

There were many good reasons for sending the Heir to the Throne to Gordonstoun, besides the fact that his father 'enjoyed' his time there, although Eton would perhaps have been a more obvious choice. Several members of the Royal Family had been there including the Duke of Gloucester and his two sons, the present Duke of Kent and his brother, Lord Harewood and Gerald Lascelles, the Earl of Athlone (Queen Mary's brother) and his son and grandson. Recent additions to the family such as Lord Snowdon and (presently) Angus Ogilvy were Etonians, and many Bowes-Lyons had spent their formative years in the school's top hats and morning tails. The disadvantage of Eton from the Prince of Wales's point of view was that it was considered too privileged an environment. It was better public relations to subject the Heir to the Throne to the popular conception of Gordonstoun's cold baths and early morning runs, which would inspire some public sympathy rather than allow him to grow up in the more cultured atmosphere of Eton College. Besides, Eton was near Windsor and that meant too near home. The Prince could have been a regular visitor to Royal Lodge, where the Queen Mother lived. The Prince and his grandmother are devoted to one another, and it would have been difficult to resist Sunday lunches there with friends, an afternoon of swimming in the Windsor Castle pool, tea on the lawn and back to the college for evening chapel. It would also have been more difficult to avoid the attentions of the press. Etonians grow used to batteries of cameras aimed at them from tourist-packed buses but the sight of the Heir to the Throne in pinstripes and tails, clutching a pile of books under his arm, would have been too good to miss. It was hoped that the four hundred miles between Fleet Street and Gordonstoun would prove a deterrent to all but the hardiest reporters and photographers.

Kurt Hahn, Founder and Headmaster of Gordonstoun.

Gordonstoun was founded in 1933 by Kurt Hahn, when he was forced to leave Germany under pressure from the Nazis. Previously the Headmaster of Salem School on the shores of Lake Constance, Hahn arrived in Morayshire with about thirty pupils, one of whom was Prince Philip. Born in Berlin in 1886 Kurt Hahn was a great innovator in education, and not only founded Gordonstoun but introduced many theories which have now become an accepted part of modern youth training. He was the instigator of a County Badge Scheme which was the precursor of the Duke of Edinburgh Award Scheme, an Outward Bound Sea School, of which there were to be nineteen by 1966. He was closely involved on a project for 'Atlantic Colleges' which are international sixth form boarding schools attracting children from all parts of the free world. The first one was the model for the United World Colleges, of which Prince Charles is now President.

Kurt Hahn's theory was that self reliance and self confidence made a good citizen. The development of these qualities depended on a sound body. His pupils were trained to achieve athletic standards gradually. Hahn believed that much was possible for those who tried and trained. *Plus est en vous* is the school motto. Thus boys took part in local community service, ran a school fire-brigade, a mountain rescue team, and a coastguard service. By co-operating with the local community, and by rescuing lives, they learned respect for their fellow humans. Hahn also believed in intellectual studies but was a fervent opponent of over specialization. He was also opposed to what he called 'spectatoritis'. He found that the appeal 'You are needed' seldom failed. A Prince has many responsibilities to his subjects, and there is much to be said in favour of a training which has enabled him in later years to rise voluntarily from his bed at an early hour, and fulfil the exacting demands of a royal schedule punctually in a spirit of general well-doing.

Whether the system would bring out the talents of, say, a Yehudi Menuhin is open to doubt. The tuning up of the healthy body to maximum service may well subordinate other possibilities.

It was during his Gordonstoun days that the competitive spirit first became apparent in the Duke of Edinburgh. He became captain of the school and of the hockey and cricket teams – 'anyone who could hold a bat was in,' claimed the Duke. He also earned the right to sail an open boat in the Moray Firth unsupervised. He enjoyed his time there. Kurt Hahn wrote of him during his last term: 'Prince Philip's leadership qualities are most noticeable, though marred at times by impatience and intolerance. He is a good school guardian, feeling deep concern about the unwritten laws entrusted to his keeping.'

The Prince of Wales was driven to Gordonstoun by his father on May Day 1962. Not everyone had as happy memories of the school as the Duke of Edinburgh. Lord Rudolf Russell, younger son of the Duke of Bedford, who had curtailed his stay there by running away, told newsmen 'My heart bleeds for him. My only recollections are of

Prince Charles arriving home from Gordonstoun for the Christmas holidays in December 1962. The picture was taken at 6.15 a.m. soon after the Prince alighted from the overnight train.

complete horror.' It was not Prince Charles's first visit, as he had toured the establishment during the previous term, 'before being incarcerated', as he put it. He was greeted by the Headmaster, Robert Chew, Hahn's successor, who reiterated the now famous phrase: 'The Prince joins in everything and has no special privileges.' He was installed in Windmill Lodge, the house of Robert Whitby. He shared a dormitory, famed for its bleakness – bare wooden floorboards, unpainted walls, beds as the only furniture of the room, and three naked light-bulbs hanging at intervals from the ceiling. Clothes were kept in locker rooms and private study was done in special huts shared with other boys.

The daily routine, unaltered summer and winter alike, was spartan to say the least. At 6.45 a.m. the 'waker', a boy whose turn it was to ensure he did not oversleep but rose before his colleagues, sounded a bell to rouse the sleeping house. Events then moved swiftly. At 7.00,

Prince Charles leaving the Braemar Gathering. The Queen Mother's car follows the Queen's.

there took place 'an easy run round the garden, followed by wash and cold shower.' Breakfast appeared at 8.15, juniors waiting at table. At 8.55 morning prayers were said. Class began at 9.10, and consisted of five forty-minute periods, but one of these tended to be a training-break, that is to say running, jumping, discus and javelin throwing, assault course and so on, under the instruction of the P.T. Master. Lunch was at 1.20 followed by a rest period: boys lay on their backs either listening to music or reading. Afternoon activities commenced at 2.30. For three days in the week, games were played – rugger and hockey in the winter, cricket, lawn tennis or athletics in the summer. The games period also included seamanship and practical estate work, all according to the individual boy's programme. One afternoon a week was devoted to training in one of the special community services: coast guard watchers, sea cadets, army cadets, scouts, fire service, mountain rescue or surf life saving. Another afternoon and an evening were reserved for individual projects, selected by the boys themselves and assessed at the end of the year. Matches were played and expeditions undertaken on Saturday afternoons, and each boy on the training plan was allowed one free afternoon. At 4.00 the boys took a warm bath followed by a cold shower, put on their evening school uniform and had tea. After tea there were two more classes or tutorial periods. Supper was served at 6.20, followed by prep done in Houses, or in groups known as Societies. Bedtime was at 9.15 and the rule of silence had to be observed for five minutes. The weary souls were returned to the world of darkness at 9.30.

The school did not have a system of fagging, since all chores were done for the good of the community at large. Prince Charles, therefore, did his share of waiting at table, weeding the garden, repairing fences, chopping logs, laying bricks, cleaning class-rooms, besides making his bed and cleaning his shoes. The emptying of the house dustbin was one chore designed to bring him down to earth, and foreshadowed his appearance in dustbins in Cambridge revues.

It was during his first year at Gordonstoun that Prince Charles, then aged fourteen, became involved in the famous cherry brandy incident. In June 1963 he was a member of the crew of a Bermuda rigged yacht named Pinta, which was cruising the Outer Hebrides for a week. The yacht berthed at Stornoway and its crew disembarked for a meal and a visit to the cinema. Seated in the hotel, Prince Charles became increasingly annoyed by a group of determined voyeurs, who persisted in scrutinizing his eating. He decided to take refuge in the bar. Here is his account of what occurred:

'Having never been into a bar before, the first thing I thought of doing was having a drink of course. It seemed the most sensible thing. And being terrified, not knowing what to do, I said the first drink that came into my head, which happened to be cherry brandy, because I'd drunk it before when it was cold, out shooting. And hardly had I taken a sip when the whole world exploded round my ears.'

He later told Jack de Manio:

'I thought it was the end of the earth. I was all ready to pack my bags and leave for Siberia or wherever.'

The incident was observed by a freelance woman journalist, dubbed 'that dreadful woman' by the Prince, and was soon splashed across the front pages of the world's newspapers. Prince Charles had not only broken school rules but also the law of the land, for under the Licensing (Scotland) Act of 1959 it is an offence for any person under the age of eighteen to buy or consume excisable liquor on licensed premises. There was some speculation as to what punishment would be meted out to the Prince. From what we know, it appears that he was summoned to the Headmaster's study. Later on, Mr Chew's only comment was: 'The incident is closed.' The Headmaster had, in fact, revoked Prince Charles's junior training plan and he had to spend the rest of the term winning it back. It was, of course, a splendid excuse for the teetotallers of Great Britain to raise an outcry.

This incident was not the first to provoke criticism of the Prince's conduct that year. He had been censured by the League of Cruel Sports for shooting a stag, and attacked by a minister of the Free Church of Scotland for skiing with other Gordonstoun boys on a Sunday.

A year later, in September 1964, another incident occurred which soon became world news. The Prince of Wales's exercise book disappeared and was presumed stolen. Mr Chew called the police and a search began. The book was found in Lancashire, but not until it had progressed through the offices of a number of press agencies and several Xerox copies had been made. Eventually it was published in *Der Stern* in contravention of the laws of international copyright.

There was a rumour that Prince Charles had sold it for cash. According to another theory, his housemaster had sold it for a large sum of money in the pub in Elgin. He, like the Prince, vehemently denied having done so. The mystery was never fully solved, although the Prince maintains that someone must have come from London to take possession of it. *Der Stern* was willing to pay £1,000 for the first serialisation and subsequent sales were said to have raised £4,000. The essays were of no greater interest or intellectual prowess than any that might have been written by an average sixteen year old. The incident caused some speculation about the financial affairs of Prince Charles. The general public had to be reassured by the Press Office that Prince Charles had adequate pocket money. In fact, as Bernard Harris revealed in the *Sunday Express,* Prince Charles is the landlord of some 140,000 acres, and is therefore 'one of the largest property tycoons in Britain'. The Duchy of Cornwall includes property in the Scilly Isles and in Cornwall as well as other parts of the West Country. It also owns Dartmoor Prison, oyster beds in the Helford river, some disused Cornish tinmines, some granite quarries in Devon, and a preparatory school in Gloucestershire. Any wreck that comes to grief on the Cornish coast becomes the property of the Duchy, and it can claim money left by people who die intestate in Cornwall and have no known relatives. The Duchy also owns forty valuable acres in London was averaging £90,000 a year in revenue. A ninth part of its income was to go to Prince Charles until he reached eighteen. After that he was to receive £30,000 year until he reached the age of twenty-one. This meant that in 1969 the Prince would have a capital sum of about £240,000. By 1964 the Duchy

Prince Charles in a sleigh in Tarasp, Switzerland in January 1963. He was staying with Prince Ludwig of Hesse in order to learn how to ski.

of Cornwall was reckoned to be bringing a sum in the region of £150,000 a year in revenue. Therefore the capital sum owned by the Prince was likely to be well over £300,000. The cost of his education and maintenance was of course paid for from this source.

Meanwhile Prince Charles developed a number of recreations. He acquired a life-saving certificate, practised surfing, undertook a daunting canoe expedition and entered into the junior training plan. He enrolled in the Combined Cadet Force, spending two years in the army section and his final days at the school in the naval, joining the school's coastguard unit. He spent some weeks at H.M.S. Vernon, the Navy's training camp at Portsmouth and acquired a foretaste of naval life and especially of anti-submarine warfare. He became a student of Archaeology and Anthropology, spending hours in the school library and digging through tons of earth with friends in a nearby cave. He took O-levels in seven subjects passing Latin, French, History, English language and literature, but had to retake Mathematics and Physics several times.

In due course he graduated to the second training plan, which is tougher and involves more self-discipline. At this time he took up polo, played the trumpet in the school orchestra and sang in the school choir. He surrendered the trumpet in deference to a German lady violinist. She had been teaching music at the school since the days of the Duke of Edinburgh and was known as a force to be reckoned with in the

Prince Charles leaving a fishing-tackle shop in Ballater in September 1964.

Prince Charles at London Airport in April 1964. Journalists wondered if he had adopted a 'beatle' hairstyle but officials hastily pointed out that he was merely windswept.

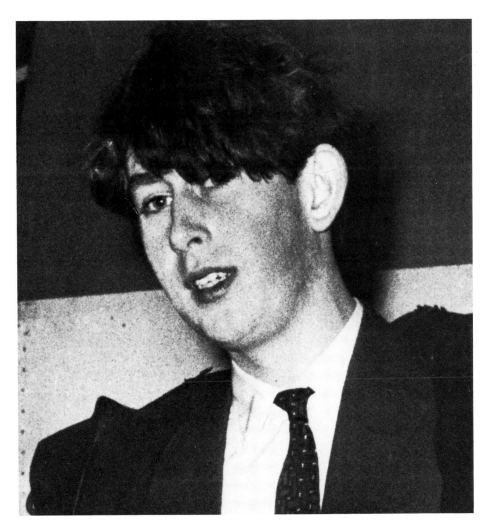

power-structure of the orchestra. She used to turn round and shout 'Ach! Zose trumpets! Ach! Zose trumpets! Stawp zose trumpets!' She won the battle and the Prince took up the cello instead. He said later:

'It had such a rich deep sound. One night I was at the Festival Hall and I heard Jacqueline Dupré playing with her husband, Daniel Barenboim. I'd never heard sounds like it. I said "I must try this." So I did, but I couldn't keep it up. I remember playing in a performance of Beethoven's Fifth one night. It was a wonderful experience, but I couldn't play concentratedly enough to avoid being confused.'

The Prince of Wales also continued his acting career. Beginning with a minor role in Gilbert and Sullivan's Patience he graduated to the lead part in Macbeth for the Christmas production of 1965. Here again he was following in his father's footsteps, though this time Prince Charles went further. The Duke of Edinburgh, on the grounds that 'there was nobody else who could be trusted to enter on horseback and not fall off' had played the 'two-lines-and-a-spit' part of Donalbain in an open air production of Macbeth when he was at the school. The Prince of Wales, wearing a wig and beard, performed an excellent Macbeth, in the presence of his parents, just a fortnight after his seventeenth birthday. Furthermore, his voice, now in the bass key, was employed in the choruses of Britten's Saint Nicholas, Elgar's Dream of Gerontius, and the Bach B Minor Mass. Finally, Prince Charles competed for the Duke of Edinburgh's Award Scheme, winning a Bronze medal in 1964 and a Silver one in 1965. He did this by qualifying in first aid, by mountaineering in the Cairngorms, by producing some pottery, and by regularly circumnavigating the school running track.

The Queen's procession leaving Westminster Abbey after the wedding of Princess Alexandra and Mr Angus Ogilvy in April 1963. The Duke of Edinburgh, The Queen and Prince Charles are followed by the Queen Mother, King Olav of Norway and Queen Frederika of Greece and by Queen Louise of Sweden, Queen Ingrid of Denmark and Princess Anne-Marie of Denmark (later Queen of Greece).

Queen Louise died in 1965 and Queen Frederika in 1981.

Prince Juan Carlos and Princess Sophia of Spain (now The King and Queen of Spain) with Prince Charles at a reception during the wedding celebrations of Princess Anne-Marie of Denmark and King Constantine of Greece in Athens in September 1964.

Besides his school activities the Prince of Wales was beginning to be seen on public occasions. His besuited or kilted figure, carnation in buttonhole, had been in evidence at the various royal weddings of the early sixties. In September 1964 he travelled to Athens to attend the wedding of his second cousin, King Constantine, to Princess Anne-Marie of Denmark. He was one of the ten people chosen to take turns in holding the traditional gold crowns above the bride's and bridegroom's heads during the ceremony. Unfortunately the strain was too much for him, and when he began to flag, Queen Frederika ever-ready to exert influence over young princes (albeit for good), stepped forward to rescue him.

Shortly after the wedding Prince Charles went out on a raft with Princess Anne, Crown Prince Carl Gustaf of Sweden and some German cousins. Despite special measures taken by the Greek police, three French journalists succeeded in evading the cordon and invading the privacy of the sunbathers. Prince Charles was rapidly learning how intrusive the press could be and the Duke of Edinburgh's relationship with newsmen was known to have been less than cordial on several occasions. The Prince decided to retaliate and three men were duly tipped into the Aegean Sea. The photographers were indignant about this and voiced their disapproval in several French newspapers. They were also able to release the photographs they had taken, the film having survived their impromptu bathe. Reginald Bosanquet once asked the Duke of Edinburgh how he had coped with the American press:

'Not too badly on the whole, but I was a bit fed up with the chaps who kept pushing microphones in my face.'
'I gather you suggested what one might do with his?'
'Yes and I hope he did.'

Prince Charles during his last term at Gordonstoun in 1964.

Australian Adventure

In January of 1965 Prince Charles attended the only state occasion which was considered sufficiently important to take him away from his studies. He was present with almost the entire Royal Family at the State Funeral of Sir Winston Churchill. He wore a huge black overcoat but no top-hat. He looked perhaps a little too glum, but early photographs often caught him like this. The sight of approaching photographers alarmed him and he withdrew into himself.

Nowadays however, the Prince of Wales takes the attitude that it is one of his jobs to keep the press happy, and he copes with them very well. He even succeeded, quite unintentionally, in putting down Bernard Levin at a lunch at New Printing House Square in July 1977. The dapper Levin apologised that he would have to leave early in order to review a play at Stratford. 'Oh!', said the Prince to the delight of Levin's colleagues, 'I thought opera was your thing.'

The Royal Family on the steps of St Paul's Cathedral after the State Funeral of Sir Winston Churchill in January 1965.

Prince Charles undertook his first royal duty at a garden party at Holyroodhouse, during a six day stay there by the Queen and the Duke of Edinburgh in June 1965. He stood beside his parents and shook the proffered hands of hundreds of Scottish and Commonwealth students. One girl missed the handshake and was summoned back for a quick grip with the call: 'Hi! Wait a moment!' The Prince was pursued by an eager reporter from the *New York Times*, who hailed this first duty with the headline:

PRINCE CHARLES A SOCIAL SUCCESS: HE'S JUST A CHIP OFF THE OLD BLOCK: BRITAIN'S ROYAL HEIR SHOWS FATHER'S CHARMING WAYS IN MEETING THE PUBLIC: PRINCE OF WALES LIFE OF THE PARTY: TAKES AFTER DAD.

Prince Charles enjoyed himself so much that he only just got back to the Palace in time for the National Anthem which brought the curtain down on that particular party.

The 7th Earl Stanhope standing in front of his portrait by James Gunn at Chevening in 1959. The silver ship was a wedding present from the Earl of Rosebery.

Among the important events of 1965, one, which later proved to be a damp squib, was an invitation from Earl Stanhope to visit his seventeenth-century home, Chevening Manor in Kent. The 7th Earl Stanhope was a widower, who had been Lord President of the Council and Leader of the House of Lords. When Winston Churchill became Prime Minister in 1940, the Earl had been dropped from the cabinet. As he had no heir, he decided to leave Chevening, with its 3,500 acre estate and an endowment of £250,000, to the nation. As early as 1943 he discussed the matter with Churchill, but it dawned on him that the Prime Minister might think he was using his gift as a bribe to return him to Cabinet office. Lord Stanhope declared, as he himself wrote 'with a bitterness that startled me as much as him' that he never wished to return to public life. For this reason he declined the offer of the Lord-Lieutenancy of Kent. Negotiations about the handing over of the estate continued and by 1959 the Chevening Estate Act was passed. Under its terms the house could be occupied by a member of the Royal Family (descended from King George VI), the Prime Minister of the day, some Cabinet minister, or by a diplomat. In 1965 Lord Stanhope wrote that he hoped Chevening could be used as a private residence. He observed that since the Second World War London had altered greatly and that Buckingham Palace was now overlooked from all sides and lacked privacy. He continued:

'It would, therefore, be of advantage for the Heir to the Throne to have a residence within easy reach of London. I need hardly say that I should warmly welcome such a future for this old house, which would then once again become home instead of being occupied by a succession of Ministers, who might, and probably would, change at short intervals . . .'

The Prince of Wales paid his first visit to the house in 1965 and the Earl showed him round. Afterwards he said 'I do hope that he will succeed me at Chevening.' Each year Lord Stanhope took his place in St. George's Chapel for the annual Garter Ceremony. He was the Senior Knight of the Garter but did not walk in the procession because he had lost his leg below the knee and was therefore allowed to drive down to the South Door of St. George's before the Procession started. In August 1967, Prince Charles paid Lord Stanhope a second visit on his way to stay with the Brabournes. The old Earl showed him some family papers and the portraits of his predecessors in the dining-room. After the visit, he felt sure that Prince Charles would one day live at Chevening, and his worries about the lack of interest of the Royal Family dissolved. A week later, on 15 August, he died peacefully in his sleep at the age of 86. His death denied him both joy and disappointment. By a year he missed the installation of Prince Charles as a Knight of the Garter. He would have watched the procession from the south door. He would have been pleased to hear that Prince Charles had decided in 1974 to take up residence at Chevening and elated to see the Prince supervising the modernisation of his future home. But then in 1980 his fervent hope would have been dashed. For Prince Charles decided to live in Gloucestershire and handed Chevening back to the trustees. In 1974 Prince Charles had hoped to save Chevening from becoming 'a lifeless museum'. Sadly this may now be its fate.

The second important event during that period was a dinner held at Buckingham Palace, shortly before Christmas. It had already been announced that Prince Charles would be spending a term in Australia at the Geelong Church of England Grammar School in January 1966, and the purpose of this dinner was to discuss his academic future. The five wise men invited were: Dr. Michael Ramsey, the Archbishop of Canterbury; Harold Wilson, the Prime Minister; Earl Mountbatten of Burma, Professor Sir Charles Wilson, Principal and Vice-Chancellor of Glasgow University and Chairman of the Committee of Vice-Chancellors; and the Dean of Windsor, the Very Reverend Robin Woods, who had recently instructed Prince Charles for confirmation. After dinner they formed a committee in order to make a recommendation to the Queen. It was agreed that the Prince should go to university, possibly to more than one, and that he should complete his course there before entering one of the Services. Prince Philip later revealed in an interview that one of the purposes of the meeting was to find out if they agreed the Prince should go to university 'even if perhaps he wasn't 100 per cent qualified'. They also discussed a possible programme for him. He had paid particular attention to History at Gordonstoun, and Prince Philip thought he should continue with that. His father also hoped that the Prince's course would include 'a number of fringe subjects and things which it will be valuable for him to have studied, rather than that he should become an academic historian.'

The result of the meeting was that the Prince's future was pointed in the direction of university, without any final decisions being taken for the time being. Within a month he was on his way to Australia for his stay at Geelong.

Leaving home was never pleasant for Prince Charles 'it was a very sad moment, of course, leaving England, seeing one's father and sister standing on the tarmac and waving one goodbye but I found the moment I was in the air it was much better.' He was accompanied by Squadron-Leader David Checketts, one of the Duke of Edinburgh's Equerries, who later became the Prince's first Private Secretary.

Prince Charles found himself at Timbertop, an outpost of Geelong, set in naturally primitive surroundings on the slopes of the Great Dividing Range. Geelong boys, who came from all walks of life with the common factor that their parents could afford the fees, spent what a former headmaster called 'the spotty year' at Timbertop, living in tiny huts and eating in a communal dining-room. They had to look after themselves, very much in the Gordonstoun tradition though as Prince Charles pointed out it was 'a very rigorous life . . .tougher than Gordonstoun.' Boys cut up gumtree and eucalyptus logs for the school kitchen, using a bushman's saw, often in a temperature of 100 F. They

cleaned out pig-sties and fly-traps, which Prince Charles described as 'revolting glass bowls seething with flies and very ancient meat'. Twice a week they made two 3½ mile runs up the steep sides of mountains, and they indulged in wheel barrow races, tree climbing, Inca races (in which fifteen boys carried a log over a mile course), and a variety of other rough unorganised games. Every weekend they set off for two days in the bush, carrying camping equipment, which included grey woollen blankets identical to those used in Melbourne's prison. 'You sort of ran around amongst the kangaroos' said Prince Charles. Then once a term there was a four day hike into the bush. The routine of Timbertop was such a strange legend to outsiders that Prince Charles was able to employ his sense of humour in relating strange tales of his activities there. he once nearly convinced some other Australians that he took part in kangaroo rustling. 'We performed this act by creeping up on them from behind, grabbing them by the tail and flicking them over onto their backs, where you had them at your mercy' he explained mischievously.

Prince Charles was two years older than most of his Australian contemporaries which was to his advantage. Time spent on study was left to the individual and in his case he brought with him the requisite books for his French and History A-levels. He worked hard, and the only major distraction was his fishing. He loved to roam through the countryside looking for good fishing spots. Prince Charles recalled that his Australian contemporaries had been very kind to him, and had not taken the mickey out of him at all. He also rather enjoyed the distant cry of 'Oh, Pommy Bastard' that followed his appearance in the unit one night with an umbrella in his hand.

He arrived at the school at a time when Donald Horne was having an all-time success with a book called *The Lucky Country* in which he advocated the need for Australia to break away from her old ties and to discontinue her allegiance to the Queen. Yet the press seemed fascinated by Prince Charles and his activities. Whenever he emerged in a public place, Australians greeted him with cries such as 'Good on you, Charlie.' There was a healthy feeling about the place that every effort should be employed to make a good Australian of him. 'You are judged there on how people see you, and feel about you,' said Prince Charles, who described Australia in 1969 as 'the most wonderful experience I've ever had, I think.' He said later that it was Australia that really got him over his shyness.

In March 1966 Prince Charles was allowed to join the Queen Mother at the beginning of her Australian tour and they spent two days together in the Snowy Mountains. On another occasion he travelled 42 miles to see a performance of *The Flies* by Melbourne University students. In May he set out with nineteen fellow students to visit Papua, New Guinea. One port of call was Wedau, a small village near Dogura Cathedral on Goodenough Bay. Here he was able to observe various aspects of missionary work and the way in which primitive man copes with being brought into sudden contact with the twentieth century. At a time which, according to the Dean of Windsor, was for Prince Charles 'the most formative period of his spiritual development' it is interesting to note that he was deeply impressed by the Church at Dogura, its freshness and sincerity. By going to a place where Christianity was appearing for the first time, Prince Charles found he could 'enter into the whole spirit of it wholeheartedly.' Furthermore, on the subject of religion, Prince Charles is said to be very aware of the changes taking place in the Church of England. One of the Queen's senior clergymen prophesied that within the next fifty years the Protestant Church would be united, the Roman Catholic and Anglican Churches reconciled, and that the monarchy would be free to cast off some of its more out-dated religious fetters. Hopefully this would include the Act of Settlement.

Other delights in store for him in New Guinea were his installation by a tribal chief as a 'successful fighting man of great courage'. As a sign of his new dignity, a necklace of boars' and dogs' teeth was placed round his neck. He witnessed some wild native dancing, and he and his colleagues reciprocated by performing a reel, no doubt to the astonishment of the natives. It was his first visit to the Tropics and he found that it made him very lethargic, something which occasionally got the better of him. In 1974 the cameras caught him dozing peacefully at a ceremony during a visit to the volcanic island of Mbau, the former capital of Fiji. He held his feet six inches from the ground, but his eyes closed long enough for a clever photograph to be taken.

One particularly unforgettable occasion was a feast at a shore-side village. Suddenly the natives began to sing *God Save The Queen* and the Prince of Wales later declared: 'it was the most moving, touching thing I have ever experienced . . . the tears practically rolled down my cheeks.'

Later he toured parts of Australia with Squadron-Leader Checketts. He caught an 8 lb coral trout at Opula Bay, and observed sooty terns flying in North Queensland. Originally scheduled to remain for only one term at Timbertop he jumped at the opportunity to stay for a second. He remained until the late summer, flying via Auckland and Mexico to Kingston, Jamaica where he joined the Duke of Edinburgh and Princess Anne at the Empire Games. On 17 August 1966 they all flew back to Aberdeen Airport for holidays at Balmoral. On his departure from Australia the Prince wrote a message in his own hand which Squadron Leader Checketts read to waiting journalists. In it he said how much he had enjoyed his stay, how sad he was to be leaving and how he hoped he would be able to return and see the parts of the country he had missed. 'I shall now be able to visualize Australia in the most vivid terms, after such a marvellous visit.' he concluded.

The Prince of Wales had to do one more year at Gordonstoun to complete his schooling. In September 1966 he became Helper (or

The Prince of Wales and Princess Anne at polo in Jamaica in August 1966.

Right: Coming of age 1966. *Far right:* Prince Charles and Princess Anne arriving at the wedding of the (now) Duke and Duchess of Abercorn at Westminster Abbey in October 1966.

The Prince of Wales riding with two 'Charros' (Mexican cowboys) in San Juan Teotihuacan, Mexico 1966.

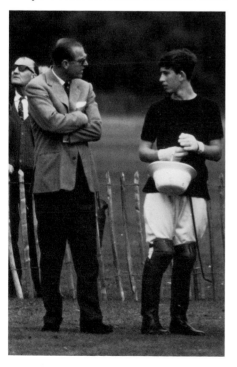

Prince Philip instructing Prince Charles at a polo match at Smith's Lawn in 1966.

Captain of House) of Windmill Lodge. The following January he became Guardian (Headboy of the whole school) as his father had been before him. His position was one of influence rather than of power, acting as intermediary between the Headmaster, the Housemasters and the boys. At this time a new confidence and maturity became evident in the Prince, and his time became increasingly occupied. In November 1966 Prince Charles came of age. In those days only the Prince of Wales achieved his majority at eighteen, other mortals being obliged to serve three more years of carefree adolescence until their time came. Prince Charles was now old enough to succeed to the throne without the need of a regency. He was also empowered to act as one of the Counsellors of State in the Queen's absence overseas. It was noted in contemporary newspaper articles that Prince Charles was almost totally unknown to the majority of his future subjects. His education had kept him out of the public eye to a quite remarkable extent, and the time had come when he should receive more public exposure. But in fact, Prince Charles went on leading a life of relative seclusion from publicity until shortly before his investiture at Caernarvon.

The final hurdle he had to face was the taking of his History and French A-levels. This was to some extent a self-imposed trial, as Cambridge, where he was now destined to go, would have accepted him without them. In July 1967 he sat the exams and in September it was announced that he had passed. Prince Charles achieved a 'distinction' in the special History paper.

Prince Charles's own view was that he was glad to have gone to Gordonstoun. He thought the general character of the education there – a balance between the physical and the mental with emphasis on self-reliance helped to produce 'a rounded human being'.

Prince Andrew salutes and Prince Charles looks on as the Royal train prepares to leave for Sandringham in December 1966.

'Gordonstoun developed my will-power and self-control, helped me to discipline myself, and I think that discipline, not in the sense of making you bath in cold water, but in the Latin sense – giving shape and form and tidiness to your life – is the most important thing your education can do.'

By the time he left school, Prince Charles had developed a marked interest in humanities and biology, particularly in anthropology and archaeology, and a fascination for medicine, but still showed a total absence of mathematical sense. He was a good horseman, better than his father, though less good as a polo-player as he was more considerate to his ponies. He had no interest in mechanical matters. Dermot Morrah thought that if he were not the Heir to the Throne he would make a good schoolmaster specializing in History and Languages.

It was the Dean of Windsor, who as a result of the 1965 dinner party, was sent on a mission to Cambridge to select a college for Prince Charles. He settled for Trinity, which had been not only his own college but that of King Edward VII, the Duke of Clarence, King George VI and the Duke of Gloucester. The announcement that Prince Charles would go there was made on 4 December 1966.

Prince Charles decided to study for an arts degree in Archaeology and Physical and Social Anthropology. Anthropology had emerged as his favourite subject and he jumped at the chance to study it at university. It was a particularly useful and appropriate subject for him to undertake as he explained:

70

'When you meet as many people as I do from different countries, different colours, different stages of social development, with different drives, you become curious about what makes men tick, and what makes different men tick differently.'

Prince Charles arrived at Trinity College on 8 October 1967. He climbed out of a small red mini, twelve minutes late due to Cambridge traffic, and was greeted by the benign-looking Master, Lord Butler of Saffron Walden. A large crowd had gathered to witness the scene and the press followed the Prince through the stages of his introduction to university life. They witnessed Arthur Prior, the deputy Head Porter hand him the key to his room and they scuttled about here and there while Robert Woods, elder son of the Dean of Windsor, took him on a conducted tour of the college. The Prince found his rooms on Staircase E, New Court, which consisted of a bed-sitting-room, a small kitchen with a sink and gas-ring, and a small bathroom. His rooms were to be looked after by a bedmaker. Here, surely, was something for the journalists, but shortly before Prince Charles's arrival, Lord Butler

The Prince of Wales with the Master, Lord Butler of Saffron Walden, in the quadrangle of Trinity College, on his first day at Cambridge in October 1967.

revealed: 'Various aspiring women are panting to receive him. But bedmakers are not allowed to be beautiful.' That evening Prince Charles took his first meal in the Elizabethan dining-hall along with 230 fellow undergraduates. He wore his college gown. The Prince later wrote that his arrival had been 'rather like a scene from the French Revolution.'

Prince Charles's studies were overseen by the Senior tutor, Dr. Denis Marrian, a Yorkshireman from Bradford. So began a life of essays and lectures, research in the college library and late night reading in his study. Academic studies were relieved by cello-playing and participation in the Dryden Society, an amateur theatre group. He also joined the Cambridge polo team and won a half blue, or 'half a shirt' as he put it. In 1969 he played in the university game against Oxford and scored the only goal, though his team was defeated 4-1.

The major difference between Prince Charles's time at Cambridge and that of King George VI was not only that he lived in college, but also that he competed for a degree on an equal basis with the other students. He was able to merge well into university life, which suited his temperament, but he was careful to avoid causing another incident such as the cherry brandy drama, or expressing controversial views which might be given unwarranted publicity. In 1969 he said that he enjoyed breaking college rules – 'half the fun is to climb in at all hours of the night'. But in fact he always preferred to exist within the bounds of the laid-down rules. His attitude is clarified in his later statement:

'I'm not a rebel. I don't get a kick out of not doing what is expected of me, or doing what is not expected of me.'

If he was to some extent a loner, it was often because he did not want to inhibit informal college activities by his presence. There was an

Four aspects of Prince Charles's life at Cambridge. *Above:* in a shop. *Left:* Gowned. *Below:* On an archaeological dig in Jersey. *Below right:* Playing polo.

amusing incident when he complained in an article of being disturbed by what he called 'the grinding note' of the early morning round of the local dustcart, of the 'head-splitting clang' of the emptying of the dustbins, and worse still, 'the monotonous jovial dustman's refrain of "O Come All Ye Faithful"'. Prince Charles did not know the dustman's name, nor did he know that he was six foot tall — thus it is fortunate that he was 'jovial'. But a gramaphone company identified the dustman and his tones were soon immortalized on record. Prince Charles also parodied the incident in a Trinity revue. Dressed in a greasy cap and a pair of jeans, he was carried on stage in a dustbin. Imitating the voice of the Goons of whom he was a great fan, Prince Charles said 'Hello, hello, hello. I empty dustbins by taking the lids off and emptying them in a dustcart, you know. Yo! Ho!'

At the end of his first year Prince Charles achieved a 66 per cent pass in Class II (Division One) of the Archaeology and Anthropology tripos. Thereafter he studied Modern History but he still made various educational visits to archaeological sites in Britain, as well as in the Dordogne, Brittany and Jersey.

In the autumn of 1967 Prince Charles began to appear at a number of important occasions in London. On 31 October he and Princess Anne took part for the first time in the Opening of Parliament. They accompanied the Queen and the Duke of Edinburgh to Westminster in the Irish State Coach, and took part in the Queen's procession through the Royal Gallery. Prince Charles sat on the Queen's right in front of the pages, and beside the be-robed figure of Lord Shackleton who stood throughout the proceedings, holding the Cap of Maintenance on a stick. Prince Charles still looked shy and placed his hands nervously on his knees as he sat in front of the august gerontocracy of the Upper House. It was on this occasion that the Queen's speech contained the momentous declaration:

The Queen and Prince Charles in the Irish State Coach on their way to the State Opening of Parliament in 1967.

'Legislation will be introduced to reduce the powers of the House of Lords and to eliminate its present hereditary basis, thereby enabling it to develop within the framework of a modern Parliamentary system . . .'

It sounded very serious at the time and although nothing hitherto has substantially changed, it was, for the Heir to the Throne, a potent example of the way the Government can use the Sovereign as a puppet.

Prince Charles celebrated his nineteenth birthday in Cambridge on 14 November and the bells peeled out from Great St. Mary's, the Cambridge University Church following a 200 year old tradition that they should do so on the birthdays of the Sovereign and of the Heir. This time the church's gardener, Walter Searle, came to Trinity College and presented Prince Charles with a rose. The Prince received it, wearing the tweed jacket and baggy trousers he habitually wore during his university days.

In December, Harold Holt, the Prime Minister of Australia, went skin-diving and was drowned. The Queen sent Prince Charles to represent her at his memorial service. Because the deceased was a Commonwealth Prime Minister, who had died in office, Harold Wilson and the Leader of the Opposition, Edward Heath, accompanied him on the memorably gruelling flights there and back with only a few hours in Australia in between. Mr. Heath recalled later that President Lyndon

Prince Charles with the Prime Minister, Mr Harold Wilson, on his way to Australia in December 1967 to attend the Memorial Service for the Prime Minister, Mr Harold Holt.

Johnson had apparently waited for Prince Charles outside Melbourne Cathedral and greeted him with the words 'It is good of you to come,' to which Prince Charles replied 'Thank you Mr President. This is my country and I welcome you to it.'

Trinity gave Prince Charles his last opportunity to do some acting. For him the environment of an establishment such as a university gave him a natural platform. It would be impossible for the Prince of Wales to take a part on the London stage, even in an era during which Prime Ministers have turned into conductors, authors of best-sellers and television personalities. Prince Charles played the part of the padré in Joe Orton's *Erpingham Camp* and another actor was presumably assured that it would be in no sense *lèse-majesté* for him to fulfil his role and hurl a custard pie at the dog-collared Prince. On another occasion he took part in about sixteen out of the forty skits of *Revu-lution*. He said it was 'the most awful type of Beyond the Fringe type of revue' and confessed to rolling about on the floor during rehearsals 'in helpless hysterics'. One part he took was that of Sir Cummerbund Overspill, a Victorian lecher. Prince Charles seized a lascivious gypsy girl and bounded from the stage calling out 'I like giving myself heirs'. He hailed back to his Timbertop days and the umbrella incident, by crossing the stage, with an umbrella above his head, announcing 'I lead a sheltered life.' These and other vignettes amused packed houses on each of the four nights it ran. The Duke of Edinburgh, Princess Anne and Princess Alexandra all came to Cambridge to see him perform. Prince Charles clearly enjoyed himself enormously. On a later occasion he said he would like to play Hamlet one day though he confessed: 'I always think of myself more as a comic character. I love doing comic parts.'

The Prince of Wales on his 19th birthday. A portrait by Cecil Beaton.

1968 saw the first appearance of the Prince of Wales in full evening dress. In the company of the Queen Mother, Princess Anne, Princess Margaret and Lord Snowdon, he attended Nureyev's performance of *The Nutcracker* at Covent Garden. Both Prince Charles and Princess Anne were gradually being introduced to public life; Princess Anne undertook her first solo royal engagement on St. David's Day 1969, and quickly became a known personality in her own right. On the same day Prince Charles had his first radio interview.

The Queen and Prince Charles walking on the royal estate at Sandringham.

A Pageant in Wales

It had been announced in 1967 that the Queen would fulfil her promise to the people of Wales and present Prince Charles to them on 1 July 1969. The arrangements for that great ceremony were put in the hands of that veteran royal ringmaster, the 16th Duke of Norfolk, whose burden was to be shared by the Constable of Caernarvon Castle, the talented and versatile Earl of Snowdon. The Prince of Wales attended a committee meeting at St James's Palace on 15 May 1968 to review the progress of the plans.

The following month, on Monday 17 June, as a fore-runner to the great spectacle at Caernarvon, Prince Charles went to Windsor to be installed as a Knight of the Garter. He was considered old enough, at the age of nineteen, to take his rightful place with the distinguished Knights, who included Viscount Portal of Hungerford, Earl Alexander of Tunis, Viscount Montgomery of Alamein and the Earl of Avon. He was surrounded by members of his family including Princess Margaret

The Prince of Wales and The Queen Mother walking in his first Garter procession in June 1968.

and the Earl of Snowdon, Princess Marina in the last few months of her life, the Duke and Duchess of Kent and Earl Mountbatten in his flowing Garter robes.

The first part of the ceremony was the investiture. The Queen, assisted by the two senior Knights, the Dukes of Norfolk and Beaufort, both appointed in 1937, placed the dark blue velvet robe over his shoulders, and invested him with the requisite insignia, star, riband, garter and collar. This ceremony was witnessed by the Knights and Officers of the Order only and was followed by a magnificent feast in the Waterloo Chamber. After lunch a colourful procession formed, headed by the Military Knights of Windsor and the Officers of Arms to lead the Knights of the Garter down the steep hill of the castle, through rows of clapping and camera-clicking spectators to the west door of St. George's Chapel. The Knights walked two by two, led by the two other recruits, Viscount De L'Isle and Viscount Amory. It was a rare occasion in 1968 for no Garter Knight was absent, though two of them, Lord Bridges and the Earl of Radnor, had to make the journey by car. Prince Charles walked with the Queen Mother and looked slightly embarrassed and rather red in the face. Nowadays he holds his head higher, and strides ahead, rather in the Mountbatten fashion. The Prince and his grandmother were followed by the Officers of the Order, the Queen and the Duke of Edinburgh.

The Prince of Wales and the other new Knights waited in the middle of what BBC Commentator Robert Hudson described as 'the mellow magnificence of the Quire' while the National Anthem was sung to the accompaniment of the blasts of trumpeters. Suddenly all went silent as the Queen announced: 'It is Our Pleasure that His Royal Highness The Prince of Wales and the Knights Companions newly Invested be Installed.' Then the 74 year old Marquess of Salisbury, Chancellor of the Order, called out in a piping voice 'His Royal Highness The Prince of Wales'. Garter King of Arms, in a scarlet cloak, conducted him to his stall on the north side of the aisle. When the other Knights had been similarly installed, the Dean of Windsor conducted the congregation through the rest of the short service. The man who had confirmed Prince Charles and helped him to explore the castle when he was younger found his voice trembling with emotion.

The process of bringing the Prince of Wales into the public eye continued during the following days when he paid his first visit to Royal Ascot, driving up the course in the Queen's carriage. In July he undertook a number of educational tours of government departments in London and South Wales to see for himself how the machinery of government worked. One such visit was to Cardiff where Prince Charles was confronted by some demonstrators bearing placards in Welsh. The Prince decided to confront the group and asked one man what his placard said. All he would say was 'Go home, Charlie', and so after a few more questions, Prince Charles gave up.

Prince Charles made his first solo flight from Bassingbourn R.A.F. airfield in a Chipmunk trainer on 14 January 1969. He had wanted to fly since he was a child, partly because his father had always done it, but also because he likes to take part in things rather than watch others doing them. Prince Charles was asked if the Queen minded him flying 'Well, possibly' he replied, 'but she's never said so if she has. I think women do tend to worry perhaps a little bit more. . . . My parents have never put anything in the way of things I've wanted to do.' He began his flying in the summer of 1968 in a Chipmunk of The Queen's Flight and progressed further with the University Air Squadron at Cambridge.

Prince Charles playing cricket.

Prince Charles in the cockpit of a Chipmunk aircraft before flying off from RAF Oakington, Cambridge.

The weather was bad for a long period of his training and so he had to put in more hours before his solo flight than was strictly necessary. He dreaded the approach of that flight but his instructor, Squadron-Leader Philip Pinney left him little time to worry about it.

'The day I went on my solo the instructor taxied to the end of the runway, having landed, and he suddenly climbed out and said, "you're on your own, mate" . . . So there I was. And I only had time to have a few butterflies in my tummy, and then I taxied off, and took off, wondering whether I could do it and the moment I was in the air it was absolutely marvellous. There was no instructor to breathe fire down the back of your neck, and the aeroplane flew much better, because he'd gone and the weight was out of the aeroplane, and I had a wonderful time. And fortunately I landed first time – that was the only worrying thing, because I had visions of myself going round and round until eventually the fuel ran out. But all was well.'

His Cambridge colleagues were not the only people to be taking an interest in Prince Charles's aeronautical exploits. As the time of the investiture approached, so many requests were received for facilities to make television programmes and films about Prince Charles's life that it was decided to make one authoritative film to be shown on television shortly before the ceremony. Richard Cawston was invited to produce the film and he started work on 8 June 1968. In all, he spent 75 days filming the Royal Family in 172 different locations. There is a memorable vignette when Prince Charles explains to his fellow undergraduates the intricacies of the equipment he wears with a thing like a loo chain that needs to be pulled at a certain moment. Prince Charles is also seen practising the cello during the Christmas holidays. His youngest brother, Prince Edward, then aged four, takes an interest which unfortunately ends in disaster. A string breaks catching the young Prince across the ear. There is a splendid scene of a lunch party on the Royal Yacht Britannia. The camera is positioned behind the Prince of Wales and unbeknown to him there is an unfortunate gap between pullover and trousers revealing some striped braces. Homely scenes were filmed at Balmoral. Prince Charles mixes a salad; the Queen helps him. 'The salad is ready,' the Queen announces. 'Good', replies Prince Philip examining a half-cooked steak, 'this, as you see, isn't.'

There is also a splendid encounter with President Richard Nixon, which took place on 25 February 1969. Now that the President's image

Prince Charles playing the cello at Cambridge.

The Prince of Wales in his Garter robes at Windsor.

has been discredited, the sight of him clasping Prince Charles's proffered hand between both of his as he grins all too widely, is viewed with eyes from which the scales have dropped. The Queen introduced her son informally as 'Charles'.

President Nixon: 'Well now, I'm so happy to see you. I was just saying to Her Majesty I've seen you on television.'
Prince Charles: 'Really? That's mutual: I've seen you sometimes.'

Diplomatic laughter ensues on all sides. Later Prince Charles returns to the theme:

'What awful television appearance of mine was this?'

And Nixon puts in a plug for his daughter which results in Tricia being invited to the investiture:

'Oh no; just the news shots you know. When you were in Australia, you know, and all the rest. And both of my daughters follow you both very very closely.'

The Royal Family film lifted the curtain on life behind the Palace walls as never before. Suddenly viewers learned that the figures they were accustomed to seeing on public occasions had private opinions and senses of humour of their own. They sprang to life on the screen and from then on the Queen, Prince Philip and others were slightly different people. Although the majority of those who saw the film would never meet their Sovereign, those that did found her very much as portrayed in it, which is certainly to the credit of Richard Cawston and his team.

Royal Family was one of several occasions in 1969 when Prince Charles ventured into the world of the media. The first was his informal radio interview with Jack de Manio, whom the Prince selected. It was broadcast on Radio 3, Radio 4 and the World Service of the BBC on St. David's Day. The Prince revealed his sense of humour from the start by asking de Manio if he had 'found this place all right'. (The interview was recorded at Buckingham Palace.) Before long, he was imitating the Goons and giving evidence of an engaging personality and of his dry sense of humour. He discussed topics ranging from his education, the cherry brandy incident and his views on student demonstration:

'I have a feeling that a lot of people are very serious about it – a lot not so serious about it, and it develops into sheer mob hysteria, which is very frightening, I would think.'

The Prince spoke in the deep and well modulated voice, which is also characteristic of the Duke of Edinburgh and the Duke of Kent. His only error was in pronouncing genealogy as geneology, but, as he said, he was no expert in the subject.

The interview was followed by a Drummond Films production in which Prince Charles talked to David Frost. In the film he talked about his attitudes, beliefs and responsibilities as Prince of Wales and the course he was taking at Aberystwyth. The film-makers found him 'relaxed and natural before the cameras'. Shortly afterwards he spoke for fifty minutes with three journalists from the Press Association, the *Liverpool Daily Post* and the *Western Mail*, and then he joined Brian Connell of Independent Television and Cliff Michelmore for a twenty-five minute interview, which, as *The Times* said, 'did much to consolidate his image.' Meanwhile a free-lance journalist called Andrew Duncan was travelling with he Royal Family taking copious notes for his book *The Reality of Monarchy*, 'not a book of which all would want to approve' as he hastens to point out in the Foreword. He gratuitously described Prince Charles as 'an awkward jug-eared teenager with a slightly lop-sided grin, quick to blush, trying to mould (him) self in the admired image of a debonair father.' He wrote critically of his education, and praised the Prince for coming out of it as a fairly normal human being. 'The fact that Charles triumphed over his upbringing was a credit to his innate good sense and ability, more than anything

Prince Charles in his first television interview with Brian Connell and Cliff Michelmore in July 1969.

else', he wrote. Finally he referred to Prince Charles as possessing the 'gentlemanly tranquillity, almost softness of an intellectual without the academic qualifications.'

In his interview with Jack de Manio, Prince Charles admitted to a certain apprehension about a course he was about to undertake at the University College of Wales, Aberystwyth. 'I expect . . . there may be one or two demonstrations, and as long as I don't get covered too much in egg and tomato I'll be all right,' he said.

A ten-day private visit to Sweden with Lord Mountbatten followed during which he was the guest of the 86 year old King Gustaf Adolf and had the opportunity to renew his acquaintance with his contemporary, Crown Prince Carl Gustaf. Prince Charles set off for Aberystwyth on 20 April. He looked a sombre figure, wearing a black tie as a sign of mourning for Queen Victoria Eugénie of Spain who had died in Lausanne the previous week.

Aberystwyth did not welcome the Prince with open arms. The Nationalists scorned the idea that he could learn Welsh and win over the Welsh in a mere eight weeks. As a protest at his coming to Wales, four students went on hunger strike, some satirical records were produced and caricatures of a strange creature named 'Carlo' appeared in shop windows. He was likely to become the target for jibes and insults, or worse. In readiness, the small town was soon swamped with plain-clothed security officers, who lurked mysteriously in pubs and other meeting places. More often than not they were greeted with the words 'Good evening officer.'

Prince Charles went to Aberystwyth on the insistence of the Welsh Office. He soon found the other students very friendly, and reckoned that they had accepted him. He joined the university surf club, which he enjoyed, and he set down to the business of learning Welsh with characteristic zeal:

'I couldn't have learned Welsh had I not been Prince of Wales, but I couldn't have worked at it as hard as I did if it hadn't been another entry into history, another way of trying to find out about people, another way of satisfying human curiosity.'

He was helped by a good ear, his powers of mimicry and numerous sessions in the university's language laboratory. He found Welsh 'a hard language, very rich and very complex'.

During his brief stay he also delved into Welsh history and literature. Prince Charles ignored the fears about his personal safety and soon began to take informal walks in the town. Small crowds used to gather to witness his arrival at college or his departure for lunch. One landlady was transported with delight when he popped into her establishment one day for an impromptu snack. A beer drinker in a local pub expressed his particular esteem for Prince Charles by declaring: 'If anybody lays a finger on that lad, they'll be strung from the nearest tree.'

The climax of his stay at the university was his address to the Youth Eisteddfod one Saturday in June. Before the meeting a local pop-singer, Dafydd Iwan, who was Chairman of the Welsh Language Society organized a demonstration. Prince Charles surprised everybody by speaking to the assembled company about 300 words of fluent Welsh, words not merely parroted but delivered with commendable fluency. That night Dafydd Iwan was hissed when he went on stage. The Welsh are an emotional race and were touched by the trouble their Prince had taken. From that moment he could do no wrong. The Mayor of

Caernarvon went so far as to declare: 'He wasn't just a boy – he was a Prince. You could have put a suit of armour on him and sent him off to Agincourt!' The prevailing feeling was that Prince Charles was 'a real *nice* boy.' When he left Aberystwyth, a huge crowd gathered to cheer him on his way.

Shortly before the investiture Prince Charles took part in another Welsh ceremony, the inauguration parade of The Royal Regiment of Wales of which he had been appointed Colonel-in-Chief. The regiment was formed by the recent amalgamation of the Welsh Regiment and the South Wales Borderers. Prince Charles wore the Colonel-in-Chief's uniform with the riband and star of the Garter and his Coronation medal. He took the salute at the parade, presented the new colours to the 1st Battalion and accepted the Freedom of the City of Cardiff on behalf of the regiment, again speaking in Welsh. The parade was followed by a civic luncheon and an evening reception. Another version of the uniform he wore that day was made for the first wax effigy of him to appear in Madame Tussaud's.

Prince Charles taking the salute at Cardiff Castle in June 1969.

A special investiture stamp designed by David Gentleman.

The Prince of Wales in the uniform of Colonel-in-Chief of the Royal Regiment of Wales.

The weeks that preceded the investiture were rife with speculation, and controversy. The government had allotted £200,000 for the ceremony. Loyal royalists thought it was not enough, while republicans declared it a ludicrous waste of money. The Duke of Norfolk felt that with another £50,000–100,000 he could have introduced what he called 'a spot more glamour' and he was quoted as saying: 'There will be no monkeying about in the name of modernization.'

While the Heralds and Pursuivants received the gentlemen of the press in the awe-inspiring sanctum of the College of Arms, the Duke of Norfolk and Lord Snowdon set about creating a magnificent spectacle in the craggy ruins of Caernarvon Castle. In a year when Concorde streaked over Buckingham Palace at 320 miles per hour to celebrate the Queen's Official Birthday, and three intrepid astronauts across the Atlantic were on the point of making 'one small step for a man, one giant leap for mankind', it was something of an anachronism to dress the Prince of Wales in purple velvet and make him promise to become the Queen's 'liege man of life and limb' and 'to live and die against all manner of folk.' However, in a curiously British way, the ceremony attracted audience ratings which competed well with those of the moon-lading three weeks later and cost a mere £200,000 in comparison to £10,000 million.

The purple velvet robe Prince Charles was to wear remained a secret until just before the ceremony. 'Some people say it's a lounge suit and others say it will be the same as what my great-uncle wore at his investiture. But it remains to be seen', Prince Charles declared in March. His great-uncle, the Duke of Windsor, who had been the first Prince of Wales in recent times to be invested at Caernarvon, was still alive and living in Paris. He joined the speculation in an exclusive article for *McCall's* magazine. He described the satin breeches, and purple mantle he had been made to wear and commented:

'I have no idea how my great-nephew will be dressed for his investiture, but I hope that whatever he will wear will be simpler and more comfortable.'

Prince Charles commented that he was not as apprehensive about the investiture as the Duke of Windsor had been because he was two years older. He added:

'I look upon it, I think, as being a meaningful ceremony. I shall also be glad when it is over, because, having spent a year in the midst of controversy and talk, between one side and another, it has become a friction point for many people.'

Meanwhile the Snowdon–Norfolk team was working surprisingly well together. The ceremony was to take place in the open air with the Earl overseeing the designs, and the Duke the ceremonial.

This was the first major state occasion which, from the outset, took account of an expected 500 million television viewers. The number of guests which had been 11,000 in 1911 was reduced to 4,000, and television cameras and their operators appropriated every available turret of the castle, while cables wriggled all over the crenellated walls. Colour television, a recent innovation, was to relay the ceremony in all its splendour.

Lord Snowdon brought in Carl Toms and John Pound to work with him as designers. 'I tried to make it as simple as possible' he said 'to let the castle speak for itself and have the dais as a kind of theatre in the round so it would read well on colour television.' The dais stood

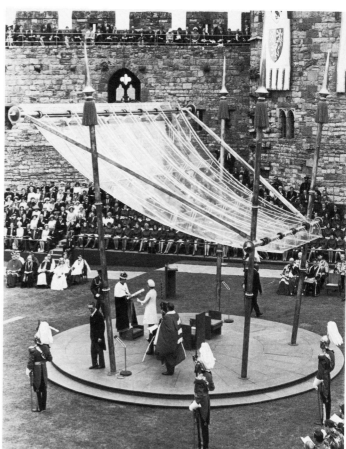

Scenes of the Investiture of the Prince of Wales at Caernarvon Castle on 1 July 1969.

beneath a see-through acrylic canopy supported by four steel lances. There were thrones for the Queen, the Duke of Edinburgh and Prince Charles. Other members of the Royal Family and distinguished guests were to be seated on special red investiture chairs some way from the central stage, which meant that the various participants crossed the green lawn, moving into action like figures in a giant game of chess. The Duke of Norfolk was responsible for all the movements. He began by setting toy-soldiers on a plan, and progressed to rehearsals on the lawn of Buckingham Palace. There was at least one occasion during rehearsals when Lord Snowdon's sense of humour got the better of him. The Heralds were solemnly going through their paces in Caernarvon Castle while he was checking the loud speaker system in one of the towers. He severely tested their composure by switching from the ceremonial music to a Sandy Shaw record which happened to be at hand.

Dress was a mixture of ancient and modern. Some peers wore their parliamentary robes, the Duke of Edinburgh wore a Field-Marshal's uniform, and the Queen wore a day-dress and hat. Lord Snowdon designed himself a dashing bottle-green costume, which included neither hat nor sword. It suited him better than it would have done the 1911 Constable, David Lloyd-George. The Prince of Wales himself wore his Royal Regiment of Wales uniform and the Garter riband and star. As it was a 'collar day' he also wore the collar of the Order of the Garter. The late King George V and his grandfather must have turned in their graves at this impropriety. The collar of an order is never worn with the riband, so Prince Charles should have left the Kingfisher blue sash at home. Curiously, since he likes tradition, it is interesting to note that this is not the only occasion when he has erred. When he rode in the procession to St. Paul's Cathedral for the Silver Jubilee thanksgiving service in 1977 he wore the Garter collar, the riband and star of the Order of the Thistle, and the star and neck-badge of the Order of the Bath. For some reason he neglected to wear the Garter star. The Duke of Edinburgh, although he cannot attach much importance to these matters, manages to juggle stars, ribands and collars and come up with the right combination on all occasions.

The great ceremony took place in fine sunshine on 1 July. From 1.15 p.m. processions of Welsh youth, mayors, sheriffs, members of Parliament and peers wended their way through the crowd of 250,000 to their appointed places. The Prince of Wales arrived by carriage, accompanied by George Thomas, the Secretary of State for Wales. He was greeted by Lord Snowdon, and the singing of *God Bless The Prince of Wales*. He proceeded through the Castle to the Chamberlain Tower where he waited patiently, keeping in touch with the outside world by watching television. It had been the same that morning at Vaynol, home of Sir Michael Duff, where fourteen members of the Royal Family had breakfasted. Prince Charles had looked at the television and said 'It's always me. I'm getting bored with my face.'

The Queen's procession followed Prince Charles's ten minutes later. When she arrived at the dais she commanded the Duke of Norfolk to direct Garter King of Arms to fetch the Prince of Wales from his tower and, presumably, from his television set. A small procession led him to the dais headed by Wales and Chester Heralds, George Thomas and Garter. Next came the Prince flanked by his sponsors, Lord Davies of Llandinam and Lord Dynevor, and followed by other peers carrying the regalia. It was apparently amidst loosely concealed mirth at the College of Arms that Lord Heycock had been assigned the task of bearing the 32 inch Golden Rod.

The Home Secretary, James Callaghan, read the Letters Patent of 1958 in English, and the Secretary of State for Wales, George Thomas, read them in Welsh, while the Queen invested her son with the Sword, the Golden Rod, the Ring, the Coronet and the Mantle. Then Prince Charles declared:

'I, Charles, Prince of Wales, do become your liege man of life and limb and of earthly worship, and faith and truth I will bear unto you to live and die against all manner of folks.'

The Kiss of Fealty was exchanged between the Queen and her son, and then Sir Ben Bowen Thomas delivered a loyal address, to which Prince Charles replied. Five years after the investiture, Prince Charles revealed that he had been sitting on his speech and had spent an agonizing few minutes during the address extracting it from under him. A re-examination of the film of the investiture confirms this, though, luckily, it passed unnoticed at the time.

Prince Charles spoke in Welsh first and then in English. He said how deeply touched he was by the loyal address and that he had taken note of the hopes expressed in it. He spoke of Wales's heritage:

'. . . a heritage that dates back into the mists of ancient British history, that has produced many brave men, princes, poets, bards, scholars and, more recently, great singers, a very memorable Goon and eminent film-stars.'

Prince Charles has retained a certain amount of the Welsh he learned. He astonished a lady from Wales whom he happened to bump into at a walkabout in Windsor in 1975, by suddenly addressing her in Welsh.

His speech was followed by a short religious service in which the congregation recited the Lord's Prayer in English or Welsh, according to choice. Some preferred *Gweddi'r Arglwydd*. The ceremony ended with the presentation of the Prince by the Queen at the Queen's Gate, the King's Gate and the platform facing the Lower Ward of the Castle. The presentations were accompanied by specially composed fanfares by the Master of the Queen's Music, Sir Arthur Bliss, climaxing in the antiphonal fanfare.

The Royal Family leaving Caernarvon Castle after the ceremony.

A birds-eye view of the scene at Caernarvon Castle. The Prince of Wales, The Queen and The Duke of Edinburgh are seated on the central dais.

Despite initial fears of bombs and demonstrations, unscheduled incidents on the day were minimal. An egg was hurled at the Queen's landau after which the thrower was almost lynched by the crowd. There was an explosion about 400 yards from the Castle, and two men were blown up at Abergele with a bomb of their own concoction. During the next four days Prince Charles travelled throughout the Principality from Llandudno to Cardiff, staying on Britannia, visiting outdoor pursuits centres, docks, schools and receiving the honorary freedom of the City of Cardiff.

Prince Charles's investiture passed off triumphantly thanks to his sincere interest in Wales and the Welsh people and to the good-natured personality he had begun to reveal through his interviews and broadcasts. The Duke of Windsor, who watched the ceremony on television at home in Paris said he thought it was 'grand'. In a television interview shown in 1970, he said:

'I think that the monarchy could not possibly be in better hands than it is today, and especially since that wonderful ceremony at Caernarvon and the way that my great-nephew Charles is getting around. I think that the Queen knows that she has a very popular and worthy successor to follow her.'

The Prince of Wales wearing parliamentary robes and the collar of the Order of the Garter, about to take his seat in the House of Lords on 11 February 1970.

Prince Charles addressing a reception for the London Welsh Association at St James's Palace, 21 July 1969.

Service Life

This Welsh interlude had interrupted Prince Charles's studies at Cambridge and he returned to Trinity in October 1969 to complete his degree course. His final months there were increasingly interrupted by public engagements and even by a long trip to Australia and Japan. Lord Mountbatten involved him in the celebrations of the centenary of Mahatma Gandhi's birth, during which he spoke at the Albert Hall. According to Godfrey Winn, Prince Charles paid his tribute 'with an ease of manner allied to a seriousness of purpose that bode well for the future.'

On 14 November Prince Charles celebrated his twenty-first birthday. The events of that day give as good an indication of the seriousness of his character as anything. In the morning he went to the Tower of London for a forty-five minute private service of Holy Communion, in which he made an act of thanksgiving and dedicated his future life as Heir to the Throne. It was a simple act of faith and contrasted with the broadcast made by Princess Elizabeth in 1947, which now seems somewhat dated. In the evening there was a special concert at which Yehudi Menuhin played, and this was followed by a dance. Guests included King Constantine of Greece and his sister, Princess Irene, King Olav of Norway and the Prince and Princess of Lichtenstein. The Prime Minister and Mrs Wilson were there and the Queen Mother came after attending the annual Students Union Ball at London University. The other four hundred guests were mostly personal friends. Amongst them was one of the Prince's tutors at Cambridge. He had been teased by undergraduate friends that he would certainly be expected to dance with the Queen, and the poor academic, whose foot had 'no music in it', resorted to verse to express his dilemma. Late in the evening, the nightly stream of traffic that passes the Palace on its way home halted awhile to admire the firework display in the garden, on the other side of the wall.

There were two close family deaths in the last months of 1969. In October Prince Charles flew to Salem to represent the Royal Family at the funeral of his aunt, Princess Theodora, the widow of the Margrave of Baden who had been Headmaster of Salem school until it moved to Gordonstoun. On 5 December, Prince Charles's grandmother Princess Andrew of Greece, died in her sleep at Buckingham Palace at the age of 84. Princess Andrew had lived at the Palace for two years, an invalid whose presence there was not widely known about. The general public remembered her as a figure clad in a grey, monastic, full-flowing robe, occasionally to be seen in the background at royal events. To Prince

Princess Andrew of Greece.

Charles's Cambridge friends she was the handsome dark-haired old lady whose striking photograph stood on his desk. She used to tell him stirring tales of her dramatic life, and a great affection had grown between them. She had shown great personal determination: having suffered from an early age from congenital deafness, she had taught herself to lip-read in English, French, Greek and German.

As the sixties drew to a close, the Queen stated in her Christmas message:

'My own thoughts are with my older children who are entering the service of the people of this country and the Commonwealth. It is a great satisfaction and comfort to me to know that they have won a place in your affections.'

Prince Charles was much in the news during the opening months of 1970. He took an examination to qualify as a licensed private pilot, which meant that from now on he would be allowed to fly any small single engine aircraft, without an accompanying pilot. The exam covered aviation, law, flight rules and procedures and meteorology. This was followed by an oral test on air frames and engineering. He acquired what is known in the world of aeronautics as an 'A' licence.

On 11 February Prince Charles donned a parliamentary robe of red cloth with four rows of white fur, and took his seat in the House of Lords. A small procession entered the Chamber led by Black Rod and

A striking portrait of Princess Andrew of Greece on Prince Charles's desk at Trinity College, Cambridge.

Prince Charles playing polo at Smith's Lawn.

followed by Garter King of Arms, the Earl Marshal, the Lord Great Chamberlain, the Lord Privy Seal, the Lord President of the Council and a man bearing the Prince's Coronet on a velvet cushion. Prince Charles entered with his two sponsors, the Duke of Kent and the Duke of Beaufort. The Prince of Wales proceeded from the Bar of the House to where the Lord Chancellor awaited at the Woolsack, making 'the customary reverences to the Cloth of Estate'. The shyness Prince Charles had shown at his Garter installation less than two years before had disappeared. At this ceremony, according to *The Times*, 'The Prince strode into the Chamber looking for all the world as though he owned the place.' He took his oath in a confident voice and shook the Lord Chancellor's hand. There was a loud rumble of approval from the peers. Having disrobed, Prince Charles returned to the House and listened to a debate on youth from the front row of the cross-benches. On 19 February it was announced that Prince Charles would spend three of four months with the Royal Air Force reaching 'wings' standard, and then enter the Royal Navy for three or five years in September 1971. After that the Prince could serve for a further period, during which he might undertake royal duties from time to time. The Prince commented 'I am looking forward to it very much. I hope I shall not be too sea-sick.'

The Queen, the Duke of Edinburgh and Princess Anne visited Fiji and Tonga, and Prince Charles flew out to join them in New Zealand on 13 March. It was the first major overseas tour undertaken by the Prince and his sister. After a week in New Zealand the Royal Family sailed to Australia, where their imminent arrival was already attracting

Prince Charles dining at Government House, Hobart.

Prince Charles and Princess Anne in an open landrover in New Zealand in 1970.

enthusiastic comment. Vicki Peterson, staff reporter of the *Sydney Daily Telegraph* reported:

'Amid all the fuss all the ordinary Australian wants to do is get on "How y' going" terms with Liz, Phil and the kids.'

She went out into Australia Square to find out what the man in the street thought. 'I think Charlie's great' said one; 'Charles already had his corners knocked off at Geelong' said another. Other opinions suggested that Prince Charles and his sister were 'real swingers', 'everyday kids', 'young, bright and modern' and simply 'beaut'.

This particular royal tour is cited as the first on which the Queen went on a 'walk-about' although royalty-watchers can quote earlier examples. Certainly it was notable for its informality and Prince Charles was to be found one morning in open-neck shirt and pullover talking to youngsters at Coogee Beach, Sydney. From Australia he went alone to Japan to visit EXPO 70. His visit was particularly

Prince Charles seated between the Emperor and Empress of Japan during his visit to Tokyo in April 1970.

enjoyable as his cousin, Prince William of Gloucester, was living in Tokyo and working as a Second Secretary at the British Embassy. The two Princes succeeded in extracting a free evening from the gruelling schedule of royal engagements so that Prince Charles could go to dinner at Prince William's house. During the visit, Prince William, who was usually known as William to all his friends reverted temporarily to being 'His Royal Highness Prince William of Gloucester.'

There were endless receptions, of course, and here is a private account of one of them:

'I went to that reception for Prince Charles . . . poor fellow he must have been bored stiff meeting so many people. It looked a bit like a zoo there with the masses all pushing and shoving their way to get a better view! He really is exactly just like the photos only maybe slightly better looking, nice and brown from Australia and longish hair. He stands just like his father with his hands behind his back and also talks with only one side of his mouth which looks a bit odd! However he seemed quite charming and everybody that met him was very impressed.'

A different impression of the Prince's fashion of speaking was formed by PHS of *The Times* in 1977, after a preview of *Royal Heritage:*

'I have discovered that the reason the Prince speaks so indistinctly is that, in East Anglian fashion, he talks without moving his top lip. Watch programme five and you will see what I mean.'

Other mannerisms that Prince Charles has adopted or inherited include the forefinger which advances in conversation – in Hollywood this reminded them of Jimmy Cagney, although Prince Charles was too polite to poke them in the chest. Another habit of his is the quick laugh which enables him to move on to the next man in the line, the clasping and unclasping of the hands (which is sometimes audible on television), and the exploring of the left sleeve by the right hand as though searching for an imaginary handkerchief. By the time he went on the Australian trip, Prince Charles had become proficient in what Dermot Morrah described as 'the harmless subterfuges and small hypocrisies of the royal profession.' These include a ready smile and the impression that the royal person is now at last talking to the one person he has waited all his life to meet.

From Tokyo Prince Charles flew home to London and returned to Cambridge to sit his finals. In June 1970 it was announced that he had obtained a B.A. degree in History. The news that Prince Charles had succeeded in open competition with other students was enthusiastically received. Trinity had done him a lot of good. When he arrived he had been, according to the Master, Lord Butler, 'very boyish, somewhat immature and perhaps too susceptible to family influence,' but now he was thoroughly grown up. Certainly there were those at Windsor who observed a great change in the Prince and attributed it not to the tougher aspects of his education, but to Trinity. It has also been said that Prince Charles enjoyed the company of the more academic students at Cambridge, but was sadly not always able to keep pace with them. His friends, as one saw them in *Royal Family*, certainly looked more like aspiring Terry Thomases than intellectuals. Prince Charles, looking back on his education said:

'I suppose I could have gone to the local comprehensive or the local grammar, but I am not sure it would have done me much good. I think a public school gives you a great deal of self discipline and experience and responsibility, and it is this responsibility which is so worth while.'

The Prince of Wales taking part in *Quiet Flows the Don*, a revue at Trinity College, Cambridge in February 1970. Here he gives a monologue on weather forecasts entitled *Weather 'Tis Nobler.*

A prize-winning picture of the Prince of Wales and Princess Anne in Canada in July 1970.

The Duke of Windsor, who had written much about the inadequacy of his own upbringing, commented:

'I would think that he is now going out into the world to do his job far better equipped than I was at that time.'

The Queen and the Duke of Edinburgh could take some joy from hearing that one of the former protagonists in the education question was well pleased. John Grigg who had voiced so many doubts in the middle 50's wrote in 1969, 'The education of Prince Charles has shown the most striking departure from traditional habits'. Gordonstoun, he thought was 'a comparatively off-beat' public school and the stay in Australia had been 'obviously much enjoyed'. His only serious criticism was what he called 'a somewhat eccentric university career'. However, he admitted: 'From all accounts he is a naturally gregarious young man, at ease in the most varied company.' Since Prince Charles was by nature shy, and by inclination a loner, his education clearly served him well for his life of public duties.

June 1970 was a time full of changes for Great Britain. Edward Heath led the Conservatives to victory at the polls with a majority of thirty-one seats, and Harold Wilson called on the Queen, who had just come back to the Palace from a day's racing at Ascot, to tender his resignation. Ironically, that same night, 19 June, it was Mr. Heath who attended a special dinner party at Windsor for four members of the Royal Family who had celebrated their seventieth birthdays, while Mr. Wilson hastily made other plans. Indeed a week later, the programme for a ceremony to commemorate the twenty-fifth aniversary of the signing of the United Nations Charter stated that 'The Prime Minister' (un-named) would welcome the principal speaker, the Rt. Hon. Lester Pearson. Prince Charles sat beside the Queen and the Duke of Edinburgh in his role as Patron of the UK Committee for the United Nations 25th Anniversary. He also wrote a foreword to the programme in which he stressed the importance of the United Nations 'as a constant, moderating influence on the nations of the world.' On 2 July the Queen opened the new Parliament at Westminster. Prince Charles and the Duke of Edinburgh were robed, principally because the Duke had hurt his wrist playing polo and it could not travel down the sleeve of a naval uniform without considerable pain. The ceremony was memorable because Lord Mountbatten, carrying the Sword of State, appeared about to collapse. Gallantly he remained on his feet, no doubt by dexterously moving his eyes and wiggling his toes in the approved military manner. That night Prince Charles left for a visit to Canada and the United States.

The reason for his departure in advance of the Queen, the Duke of Edinburgh and Princess Anne was that it is not permitted for the Heir to the Throne to travel a long flight in the same aeroplane as the Sovereign. Leaving London in bright sunshine, the Prince soon found himself in winter conditions. Some days later when the Royal Family visited an Eskimo settlement in the Arctic circle, they stayed up to see the midnight sun at Tuktoyaktuk. Unfortunately all they could see was a gleam through black rain clouds as the weather steadily worsened, and they soon found themselves shivering in temperatures twenty degrees below zero. They escaped being stranded by a mere twenty minutes. Meanwhile eighty members of the press party were marooned and had to spend the night in a gymnasium.

After Canada Prince Charles and Princess Anne visited Washington on what was called a three day private visit as guests of the Nixon family. The President, however, did not neglect the opportunity to

The Prince of Wales with President Richard Nixon at the White House in July 1970.

make a highly formal speech of welcome on the White House lawn. Prince Charles was well received, and the American press wrote enthusiastically of his having 'oomph', 'sex appeal' and 'it'. They compared him to the Duke of Windsor who had been such a success there in his youth. Prince Charles impressed the Senators by his knowledge of American history, and asked the man who was deputed to guide him round the Capitol, why America had selected the eagle as its national bird. The guide did not know the answer but said that at first they had wanted the turkey. It was not the only occasion on which that particular guide was to be caught for the right answer. He was none other than Gerald Ford.

The visit to Washington is memorable for terrible clashes between officials and reporters. Squadron-Leader Checketts was heard to snap 'Let's have some dignity around here.' Princess Anne was visibly tired after the Canada trip and found the heat of Washington exhausting. The press turned on her with such comments as 'The Prince is full of pep, the Princess acts pooped'. Altogether the stay was strenuous. Furthermore, Prince Charles reckons it is possible that his voice was immortalized on one of President Nixon's famous tapes. He had a meeting with the President which was scheduled to last ten minutes but carried on for an hour and a half.

Prince Charles told the Diplomatic and Commonwealth Writers of Great Britain that the reason Princess Anne had been criticised was that he had been 'idiotic enough to ask why the bald eagle was the emblem.' Princess Anne had commented that she thought Gerald Ford's turkey would have been a bad choice, but she was misquoted. He added that he had been offered £10,000 by 'some nameless paragon of Fleet Street' to write the occasional article. There had been much discussion about the Royal Family's finances following some remarks by Prince Philip and so Prince Charles added 'Perhaps I should have accepted the offer and thus helped the general monetary crisis which affects some people I know rather well.'

The months between August 1970 and March 1971 when Prince Charles entered Cranwell were less hectic than the previous ones. He went to Fiji in September to represent the Queen at the Independence Celebrations and then visited the Gilbert and Ellice Islands, Bermuda and Barbados. In Bermuda, where he received a friendly welcome, he represented his mother at celebrations marking the 350th Anniversary of their Parliament. In London he took part in The Countryside in 1970 Conference and made a speech at the Guildhall, and when General de Gaulle died on 9 November he was available to go to Notre-Dame in Paris to attend a memorial service in the company of Heads of State such as the Shah of Persia, Queen Juliana of the Netherlands and President Nixon.

A month earlier he had the opportunity to make a call on his great-uncle, the Duke of Windsor. The visit took place on 1 October after a hunting holiday near Amiens with the British Ambassador, Sir Christopher Soames. Prince Charles had met his great-uncle only once before, at the funeral of Princess Marina at Windsor in 1968. He also met the enigmatic Duchess, whom he addressed as 'Aunt Wallis'. Other cousins such as Prince William of Gloucester, were occasional but always welcome guests at the Duke's table in his later years.

In January 1971 Prince Charles and Prince Philip were the victims of one of the occasional onslaughts launched by the League against Cruel Sports. The Chairman, Raymond Rowley, accused them of hypocrisy in supporting the World Wildlife Fund while still taking part in

Prince Charles addressing 5000 top company directors at the Royal Albert Hall in November 1970. His 30 minute speech earned him a standing ovation.

Prince Charles arrives at the Master Tailors Benevolent Association annual dinner in February 1971.

massive shoots at Sandringham. Lord Snowdon was praised by the League and quoted as saying 'Any idiot can be a good shot.' The Royal Family were still very sensitive to the issue of bloodsports, especially hunting. Later Princess Anne and Captain Mark Phillips weathered the storm of public criticism and are now active hunters. Recently Prince Charles has also become an enthusiast, though he remains sensitive to photographers when in pursuit of the fox. But in 1970 a reference to hunting in the Duke of Windsor's interview with Kenneth Harris was broadcast only once and then cut from future showings and edited from the recording. In it the Duke revealed that he had asked Princess Anne why she did not hunt. She replied simply 'Bloodsports.'

Further criticisms were voiced against the Prince, this time of a less serious nature. Karl Dallas, fashion editor of the *Tailor and Cutter* which had praised Prince Charles's sartorial elegance as a lad, launched an attack on his mode of dress, describing him as a representative of the cult of shabbiness practised by the English aristocracy. Mr Dallas was baffled by the Prince's habit of favouring suits with turn-ups one day, and without the next. Mr Dallas was not deceived:

'It would be pleasant to conclude that he was consciously changing back to turn-ups like the rest of his generation, but we fear that we are in fact seeing survivals of earlier suits not yet completely superseded or worn out.'

He attacked the Prince's dinner-jacket – 'a mistake' – the width and baggy seat of his trousers and the 'boxy' cut of his jacket which was thrown out of proportion by his predeliction for a wide tie. Prince Charles clearly enjoyed the criticisms enormously and arrived shortly afterwards at the annual dinner of the master Tailors' Benevolent Association wearing a tweed jacket over white tie and garter riband. 'I cannot resist sometimes taking the mickey' he said. In his speech he told the tailors that he had been variously described as 'being dressed as an out-of-work parson' and 'one of the best-dressed men in the world.' He suggested a reason for the habit he shares with his father of standing with his hands behind his back. Looking across the table to Mr. Edward Watson, who was both the Duke's and his own tailor, he said: 'He makes the sleeves so tight, we can't get our hands in front.'

In the Spring Prince Charles accompanied Princess Anne on a fortnight's visit to Kenya. He played polo, riding a mount called Christine Keeler, which prompted tired jokes from headline-seeking

Prince Charles at the Lake Nakuru National Park in Kenya with senior game warden, Joseph Mburugu.

journalists. He also undertook a four day safari in the rocky scrub and desert country north of Isiolo. He did it on foot, though camels accompanied the party to carry baggage and the occasional weary trekker.

On his return he had three important lunches to attend. He joined the editorial staff of *Punch* and carved a C on the *Punch* table. On 2 March he went through the ancient ritual of receiving the Freedom of the City of London, complete with a carriage drive through the city, a ceremony at Guildhall and a lunch at the Mansion House. The most eminent fishmonger in the land, admitted by patrimony, put in a plug for the Services in his speech:

'Surely the Services must attract a large number of duty-conscious people: otherwise who else would voluntarily subject themselves to being square-bashed, woken up at unearthly hours, shouted at by bristling sergeants and petty officers, and made to do ghastly things in force 10 gales?'

Finally Prince Charles had lunch with Mr. Heath at 10 Downing Street, after which he learned how the Prime Minister's Office functions.

On 8 March he travelled in an aircraft of the Queen's Flight to Cranwell for a five month stint with the R.A.F. He was greeted somewhat formally, but it was made clear that from then on the royal Flight-Lieuenant would be saluting all senior officers. The formal greeting is summed up in a comment by the Commandant of Cranwell, Air-Vice-Marshal Desmond Hughes: 'We are proud that a precious piece of the nation's property is being trained here.' The Prince's bedroom contained a bed, slightly too small for comfort in the best traditions of the Services. The only difference between this Flight-Lieutenant and the others was that he had no service number and received no pay. Prince Charles also had a private sitting-room where he could attend to state papers. On his first day he was seen meeting his three flat-mates, who grinned nervously as though they were about to audition for supporting roles in *Battle of Britain,* and the same day he was in the cockpit of a 500 m.p.h. Jet Provost with his instructor, Squadron-Leader Dick Johns.

The two Jet Provosts that the Prince flew were maintained to Queen's Flight standards, which were even more exacting than Cranwell's. Prince Charles achieved his solo flight after eight hours in the air, and later confessed to intense satisfaction at having mastered the Provosts. His instructor was impressed by his enthusiasm: 'Prince Charles has an absolute, complete and utter determination to do his best. I've never had a pupil like it,' but it was noted that he had only 'a

The Prince of Wales on his first day at RAF Cranwell. He is seated in the cockpit of a Jet Provost with his instructor. March 1971.

The famous parachute jump at Studland Bay, Dorset on 28 July 1971.

polite interest in technical subjects.' He mixed well with the other officers and played an April Fools Day joke on them by having an announcement made asking officers to deposit their shoes for inspection in a conspicuous place in the care of the porter. A number of shoes appeared but the joke cost the Prince a heavy round of drinks as the announcement went out on the wrong side of mid-day. Later in the year he scored ten runs for the R.A.F. in a cricket match coming out to bat on a pony he borrowed for the occasion.

A typical day at Cranwell was 10 March 1971. Prince Charles rose at 6.45 a.m., bathed and breakfasted on cornflakes, honey and milk. Shortly before 9 a.m. he cycled to the swimming pool for dinghy drill. After a short break he was taught how to break the impact of parachute landing in the gym. Before a lunch of fried steak and chips, black-currant and apple pie and cream, he tackled a work sheet. In the afternoon he was subjected to an ejector seat demonstration, and was shown how to strap himself into an aircraft. At 5 p.m. he took a work sheet home with him and at 7.30 he went out for a private engagement.

His best known achievement was a parachute jump he made on 28 July 1971, an occasion on which the Heir to the Throne was 'thrown to the air.' He made the jump from an R.A.F. Andover cruising at 1,200 feet above the sea off Dorset. As he climbed into the Andover he asked the 'hairy Flight Sergeant' if he was the chap who would push him out:

'Oh no, Sir, no, no, no, we don't do that, we just help.'

The Prince jumped and found himself upside down, with his feet caught in the rigging line. Having extricated himself from this tangle he paid attention to the unhooking of the reserve parachute and presently he landed in the sea, where within seconds he was rescued by the Royal Marines who were 'roaring around in little rubber boats.' He celebrated his safe landing with a glass of wine, speedily followed by a hot bath.

This exploit and others show a remarkably relaxed attitude to the Prince's personal safety. Earlier in the year Prince Michael of Kent had been dragged 300 yards at 65 m.p.h. after his four man bobsleigh crashed at Cervinia. Prince Michael suffered a deep gash under his chin and a badly-bruised left elbow and was in hospital for ten days. The following year, in August 1972, Prince William of Gloucester was to die in a flying accident while taking part in the Goodyear Air Race near Wolverhampton. At the inquest, his death was attributed to 'an error of judgment' and the coroner added that it was possible he had been too rash in a turn he made shortly after take-off. Prince Charles could always reply to any critics of his activities, as the Duke of Windsor had done to Lord Kitchener, that it did not matter if he was killed, as he had brothers to take his place.

On 20 August Operation Golden Eagle, the code name given to Prince Charles's R.A.F. training (and the name of his radio call sign) came to an end. At a parade watched by the Duke of Edinburgh, Prince Charles received his wings from Air Chief Marshal Sir Denis Spotswood and then father and son set off for their customary summer at Balmoral.

In September Prince Charles exchanged his Flight-Lieutenant's uniform for that of an Acting Sub-Lieutenant in the Royal Navy, and joined the Royal Naval College, Dartmouth where he undertook a six-week graduate course. Then he joined the 5440 ton guided missile destroyer, H.M.S. *Norfolk* in Gibraltar with which he served until July 1972. By Christmas time he had already served watch during a severe storm off Sardinia. In the course of the next few months he experienced conditions sixty foot under water when he spent twenty-four hours on board the submarine H.M.S. *Churchill*.

A notable break and for Prince Charles a sad one occurred when he joined the Queen and the Duke of Edinburgh on their state visit to France in May 1972. He met his parents in Provence and they visited Avignon together. At Les Baux Prince Charles admired the long dresses of the dancing-girls but commented: 'Les minijupes, c'est quand même plus pratique!' The Royal Family returned to Paris and after an afternoon's racing at Longchamp, they called at No. 4 route du

Prince William of Gloucester who was killed in a flying accident in August 1972.

The Prince of Wales receiving his wings from Air Chief Marshal Sir Denis Spotswood on 20 August 1971.

Champ d'Entrainement, the home of the Duke and Duchess of Windsor. The Duke was too ill to come down from his bedroom and when the visit was over, it was the Duchess who bravely bid farewell to the Queen outside the house, knowing that her husband had but a short while to live. Prince Charles had grown fond of his uncle and looked completely stricken as he left the house. Acute observers at the time took this as an indication that the Duke of Windsor's illness was far more serious than had been suggested. The Duke of Windsor died on 28 May, in the early morning, a mere ten days after his niece's visit. His body was taken to England to lie in state at St George's Chapel. The Queen commanded that the Birthday Parade should incorporate an act of remembrance for her uncle. Immediately the Queen arrived on the parade ground there was a roll of drums followed by a minute's silence and then another roll of drums. The pipes then played the lament, *The Flowers of the Forest*. Prince Charles, who had flown home specially from Malta, is reported to have told the Duchess of Windsor that he burst into tears when he heard it. That evening, it was Prince Charles, with Lord Mountbatten, who escorted the Duchess to St George's Chapel to see the Lying-in-State privately after the last of the 58,000 people had filed past the catafalque. They followed the coffin into the Albert Memorial Chapel where it was to rest until the funeral, two days later. Prince Charles was one of the mourners who followed the coffin at the funeral, walking behind the Duke of Edinburgh and the King of Norway. Then he flew back to Malta to rejoin his ship. He had always been particularly kind to the Duchess of Windsor and did much to

The Duke of Edinburgh, The Prince of Wales and Prince William of Gloucester following the Duke of Windsor's Coffin at the funeral in St George's Chapel in June 1972.

make her feel she was no longer ostracized. Royal Funerals tend to be dramatic and moving occasions, full use being made of the power of ceremonial, rolling of drums, dramatic organ music and beautiful singing to mark the laying to rest of a royal soul. Prince Charles has admitted to being an emotional person. He said that a certain passage in Berlioz's *L'Enfance du Christ* was 'so moving I'm reduced to tears every time.' Similarly, the funeral of the Duke of Gloucester who died in June 1974 after a long illness, included a final musical tribute, which made a deep impression on all those present in the nave. Again it was a lament, played this time by a lone piper, who walked down the south aisle as the coffin was borne down the central aisle. Even the most hardened hacks on the press-benches looked suddenly curiously mellow.

The Prince of Wales was again in England in the summer. Shortly after a polo accident after which he had seven stitches in his chin, he captained the Young England team, but they were defeated by the US Under 25 side. At Portsmouth he conducted the Queen on a tour of H.M.S. *Norfolk* and he undertook various shore courses. In July he attended Prince Richard of Gloucester's wedding to Birgitte van Deurs and all too soon afterwards the funeral of Prince William, the groom's elder brother and best man.

The Queen and the Duke of Edinburgh celebrated their Silver Wedding on 20 November with a service at Westminster Abbey and a luncheon at Guildhall. Afterwards Prince Charles, sporting a red carnation in his buttonhole and a diamond tie-pin in the design of the Prince of Wales's feathers, took part in the televised walkabout through the Barbican. In the evening he and Princess Anne gave a party for

The Queen and the Royal Family photographed at Windsor at Christmas 1971. *Back Row (standing):* Lord Snowdon, The Duke of Kent, Prince Michael, The Duke of Edinburgh, Lord St Andrews, The Prince of Wales, Prince Andrew, Angus Ogilvy and his son, James. *Seated:* Princess Margaret, The Duchess of Kent with Lord Nicholas Windsor, The Queen Mother, The Queen, Princess Anne, Marina Ogilvy and Princess Alexandra. *Seated on the floor:* Lady Sarah Armstrong-Jones, Lord Linley, Prince Edward and Lady Helen Windsor.

their parents which included an entertainment with performances by Raymond Leppard and Peter Ustinov, Benjamin Luxon and part of the Bach Choir. Both Prince Charles and Princess Anne were praised by Lord Jellicoe for their deep involvement in a wide spectrum of national affairs.

From November until March 1973 Prince Charles served with H.M.S. *Glasserton*, a coastal minesweeper. Then he transferred to H.M.S. *Minerva* until September, spending time as an assistant navigation officer in the Caribbean. On 1 May he was promoted full Lieutenant.

At the end of May Prince Charles was given sixty hours of leave. Twenty-four of these were spent in the air in order that he could join his family at Craigowan House, Balmoral for a reunion before the announcement of Princess Anne's engagement to fellow equestrian, Lieutenant Mark Phillips. That announcement was made on 29 May and diverted the attention of the press from Prince Charles for the next few months. Princess Anne was married in Westminster Abbey on 14 November 1973, the Prince's twenty-fifth birthday.

The Royal Family at Balmoral in the summer of 1972. Left to right: The Duke of Edinburgh, The Queen, Prince Andrew and Prince Edward, Princess Anne and The Prince of Wales.

Princess Anne's wedding on 14 November 1973. The Royal Family on the balcony. Left to right: Captain Mark Phillips, Princess Anne, Lady Sarah Armstrong-Jones (a bridesmaid), The Prince of Wales (whose 25th birthday it was), and The Queen.

The Prince of Wales chats with the Prime Minister of the Bahamas, Lyndon O. Pindling, at the Bahamas Independence celebrations, 10 July 1973.

Prince Charles enjoying Goon Humour with Harry Secombe (left) and Spike Milligan at the Eccentric Club, London on the publication of *More Goon Show Scripts* to which he had written a foreword, November 1973.

When naval duties permitted, Prince Charles undertook certain royal engagements. In July 1973, he represented the Queen at the Independence celebrations of the Bahamas. During the handing-over ceremony, a sun canopy collapsed on the royal party but no-one was hurt. As part of the festivities Prince Charles danced in a fiesta, staying up until the first light of dawn. Partnering Mrs. Marguerite Pindling, wife of the Prime Minister, the Prince threw himself enthusiastically into the fun of the occasion. The Daily Telegraph commented:

'Guests backed off to watch his version of a pulsating local dance called the merengue, which he performed with twisting hips and arms going like pistons.'

Prince Charles left H.M.S. *Minerva* in September, having gained his bridge watchkeeping and ocean navigating certificates. For the rest of 1973 he took the shore courses for destroyer navigating officers, divisional officers and flight deck officers. Shortly after Christmas he set off to join H.M.S. *Jupiter* in Singapore, for a spell in Australian waters, but he took time off to join the Royal Family in New Zealand for the Commonwealth Games.

Prince Charles dancing in Scotland with his cousin, Lady Sarah Armstrong-Jones.

A Life of Service

Below left:
The Prince of Wales becomes an Elder Brother of Trinity House in June 1974, in company with the other Elder Brethren who include Mr Harold Wilson, the Duke of Norfolk, Prince Philip (Master), Earl Mountbatten of Burma and Mr Edward Heath. Black mourning bands were worn due to the recent death of the Duke of Gloucester, a former Master.

Chevening, where the Prince of Wales announced in 1974 that he would live. In the event, he never took up residence at Chevening, but decided to live in Gloucestershire.

In June 1974 the Duke of Gloucester died. A few days later Prince Charles became an Elder Brother of Trinity House and in the wake of Lord Snowdon, he delivered his maiden speech in the House of Lords. The Lords was packed with Peers, and there was a gala atmosphere as Peeresses wandered about as though it were Gold Cup Day. The Press Gallery was awash with foreign representatives, who were so overcome by the royal aspect of the occasion that they rose to their feet when the Lord Chancellor entered. They were eyed with disgust by home-based pressmen.

The Duke of Kent and Lord Snowdon were on the cross-benches to hear Prince Charles make a sixteen-minute speech which called for the better co-ordination of leisure facilities to meet the challenge of what he

called 'removing the dead hand of boredom and frustration from mankind.' Prince Charles was predictably entertaining, referring to an earlier occasion when royal Dukes took part in a debate. They had attacked each other so vehemently that the House fell into silence. He promised not to employ the same tactics on his cousin, the Duke of Kent. On the subject of making a speech, he quoted: 'If a thing is worth doing it is worth doing badly' which he attributed to Oscar Wilde. That evening Frank Muir, an expert on the provenance of witty sayings, announced that it was G. K. Chesterton who had said it. 'If a thing is worth quoting, it is worth quoting badly', added Muir.

From September to December 1974 Prince Charles took a helicopter conversion course at the Royal Naval Air Station at Yeovilton. A film, *Pilot Royal,* showed him tackling a helicopter, and climbing out complaining cheerfully about how uncomfortable the cockpit was reckoning that he would have suffered from 'helicopter haemorrhoids' if he had stayed in much longer. This time 'Golden Eagle' was called 'Red Dragon'.

In the Autumn the Prince of Wales set out on a visit to Fiji and then went on to Australia. He took the opportunity to express his views on the role of monarchy in Australia when he addressed the New South Wales legislative council. He thought the British and Australian Parliamentary system was the one which came nearest to ensuring stable government. He continued:

'And I also believe that the institution of monarchy – to which rightly or wrongly I belong and which I represent to the best of my ability – is one of the strongest factors in the continuance of stable government.'

Speculation grew that Prince Charles might be appointed Governor-General, but he thought it unlikely, saying while in Melbourne:

'I suppose if there was a desire for me to accept such an office I would consider it.'

'A most horrifying expedition.' Prince Charles undergoing a commando training course in Devon in January 1975.

Earl Mountbatten of Burma with Prince Charles at the Coronation of King Birendra of Nepal in February 1975.

Prince Charles mustering cattle in South Queensland in October 1974.

In December Prince Charles headed the helicopter fly-past and passed out a qualified naval helicopter pilot. Then he sped to Wales to open Sony's new factory at Bridgend – the result of a meeting in 1970 with the Chairman of Sony in Japan at which Prince Charles suggested Wales as a possible site for a factory. 'Nobody could be more surprised than myself,' said Prince Charles 'when two years later the smile on the face of the inscrutable Japanese chairman turned into an actual factory in South Wales.' The factory provided jobs for about 250 local people, and has since been cited as one of the most efficient in Great Britain.

A 'most horrifying expedition' awaited Prince Charles in January 1975 when he underwent a commando training course near Lympstone in Devon which involved wading through rivers and tackling tree-to-tree ropes. In February it was reported that a Wessex helicopter in which he was a co-pilot had to make an emergency landing. It was the second such emergency in his helicopter flying career. Later that spring he travelled to Delhi and Nepal and attended the Coronation of King Birendra in Kathmandu.

In April he visited Canada, during which trip he dived thirty feet below the Arctic ice and returned to the surface, wearing a bowler hat. Prince Charles was very energetic throughout the visit, so much so that

Prince Charles in Arctic conditions.

a guest at a ball at Government House in Ottawa asked if he had had special injections. He scored a great hit with Margaret Trudeau, wife of Canada's trendy Prime Minister. Canada's newspapers were very impressed by the Prince and reported that Mrs Trudeau was not the only lady to find him entertaining. The *Toronto Daily Star* wrote of 'blue-rinsed matrons nearly pushing Charles's police escorts into glass-panelled walls' and reported: 'simpering women clerks dissolved into shrieking and quivering as soon as the bachelor heir to the throne touched their hands and passed by'. Furthermore, one teenage girl almost swooned when Prince Charles talked to her.

After his official ten-day visit, Prince Charles went to new Brunswick for helicopter exercises at a base near Blissville. Due to Arctic conditions in which it was impossible to shave he began to grow a beard. He retained the growth, dubbed 'Charles's bristling poser' by the *Daily Express* where he flew back to London to be installed as Great Master of the Order of the Bath in Westminster Abbey. His face went through a variety of changes in the next twenty-four hours. He felt that for the great ceremony a beard looked somewhat undignified and so 'Razor-sharp Charles' reduced it to a moustache. The experts on Queen's regulations in respect of whiskers were quick to accuse the Prince of parading in front of his Sovereign and other naval officers in flagrant contravention of naval rules. The Palace swiftly pointed out, however, that the Prince was wearing his uniform as Colonel of the Welsh Guards and was thus a military man on this occasion. Eager journalists went out into the streets to find out how the female element of London responded to the beard. 'It made him look mature' said one, 'sexy – as if he was game for anything' said another. 'I liked his beard because it hid

'Charles's bristling poser'—The Prince of Wales returns to England with a beard in May 1975. He is followed by his then Private Secretary, Squadron-Leader (now Sir) David Checketts.

The Prince of Wales photographed at Balmoral.

Prince Charles at Cowes in 1978.

Prince Charles accustoming himself to a rifle.

his weak chin! Apart from that I thought it made him look really dishy' said a third, and a fourth commented: 'He just has not got the face for a beard. I thought it looked as if he had a tidemark round his chin.'

Prince Charles strode into the Abbey wearing the crimson robe of the Great Master of the Order. He never looked more self-confident than on that day, never more like a progeny of the Mountbattens. In the course of a long ceremony he promised 'to honour God above all things' and 'to defend maidens, widows and orphans in their rights'. Prince Charles then repeated the procedure to eight new Knights, who all partially drew their swords towards the altar and re-sheathed them in unison with the new Great Master. After the service the Prince returned to the Palace where he whisked off his moustache, and prepared to rejoin H.M.S. *Hermes*, a commando ship, until June.

In the Summer Prince Charles again addressed the House of Lords in a debate on voluntary service in the community. He reported that he had established experimental youth schemes in various places and that so far the response had been 'extraordinarily encouraging.' This and his earlier speech sowed the seeds for the Queen's Silver Jubilee Appeal which was to be launched in 1977.

Royal engagements were becoming increasingly informal and adventurous. When Prince Charles decided to inspect a famous naval relic off Spithead, he thought nothing of making the fifty foot descent under water with a historian from the British Sub-Aqua Club. He stayed down for forty-seven minutes, then after a breath of fresh air went down for a second look. Later in the year he attended Papua New Guinea's Independence celebrations and not only witnessed dancing girls, but a tribal dance by 'mud men', in which almost naked warriors with faces coated in mud, demonstrated how they approach their enemies, hissing aggressively through their teeth.

Polo and Badminton. *Left:* Prince Charles with his more impressive 1976 beard.

The Prince's motor cavalcade for his arrival in the Ivory Coast during his West African tour in March 1977.

In September 1975 the Prince arrived at the Royal Naval College, Greenwich (ten minutes late due to heavy traffic) in order to begin a three month Lieutenant's course.

The following February Prince Charles took command of the 360 ton minehunter H.M.S. *Bronington*, known throughout the fleet as 'Old quarter-past-eleven' as her pennant number is 1115, and took up residence in the Captain's nine-by-seven foot cabin. A day or so later he welcomed his father aboard for tea and cucumber sandwiches and showed him round the warship.

On 21 April the Queen celebrated her fiftieth birthday with a party at Windsor, which Prince Charles attended. At that party and at the Badminton Horse Trials he again presented a bearded countenance. This time the beard had had longer to grow and was, accordingly, more impressive. Then, one Saturday in June, a now clean-shaven Prince managed to fit a game of polo in between the rehearsal for the Queen's Birthday Parade and a concert given by the Bach Choir at St. George's Chapel, after which there was a lively informal gathering on the terrace outside the Chapter Library in Windsor Castle.

During the summer he kept very much out of the news, engaged almost exclusively in naval exercises which included a twelve day NATO exercise in the North Atlantic. In July he was reunited with his family for the Olympic Games at Montreal in which Princess Anne competed and later in the summer he was elected Chancellor of the University of Wales, Cardiff in a straight fight with Dai Francis, the Communist and a former miners' leader.

The Prince's easy-going and pleasant manner was beginning to earn him considerable popularity. When the *Bronington* was in dock at

Rosyth, Prince Charles played host to the wives and families of his crew. His invitation said that he hoped the demonstrations, which included flying and machine-gun displays, would give the civilians a clearer idea of 'life at sea than can normally be extracted from your menfolk on their return home.' Prince Charles welcomed a local pin-up girl, invited aboard by the senior ratings, by enquiring if she had taken her pill. She said she had indeed taken her sea sickness tablet, adding to reporters 'He was very nice and friendly and he cracked this wee joke with me.' On another occasion when a sub-Lieutenant was prevented from being at the birth of his daughter, the Prince sent a hand-written message of congratulation to his wife apologising for detaining her husband.

One of the *Bronington*'s activities was to blow up a wartime mine. And in November she led a sea and air search for a couple who were missing from a yacht. A lifeboat, a lifebelt, a sail and a log-book were located but neither the yacht nor the man and woman were found.

Prince Charles eventing.

Prince Charles at the helm of *Eye of the Wind* when he launched Capital Radio's Operation Drake in 1978.

The Royal Family leaving the private chapel in Windsor Great Park on 6th February 1977, the actual anniversary of the Queen's Silver Jubilee. *Left to right:* The Duke of Edinburgh, The Queen, Queen Elizabeth The Queen Mother, Prince Edward, Princess Anne, Princess Margaret and Prince Charles.

Sir Peter Studd greeting The Prince of Wales as he arrived at the offices of The Queen's Silver Jubilee Appeal Council at 8 Buckingham Street in December 1976.

The Prince of Wales and friend at Cirencester Park before the Prince took part in one of the team events.

In December Prince Charles left the Royal Navy in order to be free for activities during the Queen's Silver Jubilee Year. He was given an unusual send-off at Rosyth. In the best naval tradition of humiliating a popular captain on leaving his command, the Prince was wheeled through the dockyard in a wheelchair from which his standard flew. On his lap was a lavatory seat with a roll of lavatory paper attached to it. After shaking hands with every member of the crew, he called out 'Behave yourselves, lads, when I'm gone.'

1977 was a memorable year for the Royal Family and for Great Britain. Initially, the Silver Jubilee was greeted with a general feeling of scepticism. Prince Charles himself was confronted at a Cardiff news conference by a banner proclaiming 'No money for jamborees'. He hastily explained that the Silver Jubilee Appeal he was launching was to allow individuals 'who feel affection and loyalty to the Queen after twenty-five years' to contribute to a fund for young people. In 1935 the Silver Jubilee Appeal had raised £1 million. In 1977 Prince Charles said he thought £5–10 million would be more appropriate.

The Prince of Wales or, more properly on this occasion, The Duke of Rothesay, at his installation as Knight of the Thistle at St Giles Cathedral in June 1977.

Right:
The Prince of Wales in the uniform of Commander of the Royal Navy. He wears the Garter star, The Queen's Coronation medal and aiguillettes as a Personal ADC to Her Majesty.

The Prince of Wales being made an honorary chief in Ghana during his West African tour in March 1977.

Honours fell upon him in the early months of the year. He was appointed a Commander in the Royal Navy, a Wing Commander in the R.A.F. and a Knight of the Thistle. He visited Kenya, Zaire, Ghana and the Ivory Coast.

On Sunday 24 April Prince Charles launched the Appeal in a live broadcast from Chevening House. At a time when the camera-crew of Royal Heritage were hailing him as 'one-take Wales' because of his proficiency in front of the cameras, this live talk did not bring the best out of him. Prince Charles is considerably better when addressing a live audience with the possibility of a voice from the crowd to which he can make a quick ripost. In this talk he had to read his script, and he had a curious tendency to look down at his hands as though he was checking the time. Nevertheless, even if his performance was not up to his usually high standard, his message did not fall on stony ground. Basically he was appealing for money 'to help young people help others.' He cited various examples: 'work in hospitals and homes, help for the elderly and the lonely, for the disabled or mentally handicaped, for the deprived and sick children, work to improve the local environment, rescue services, adventure projects and other forms of leadership training.' A week later it was reported that money was flooding in so fast that the bank could not even give a running total. Throughout the year purchasers of tickets to a wide variety of fund-raising events, from concerts and sporting occasions to an elaborate dusk-to-dawn party in Berkeley Square, supported the Appeal, sometimes unwittingly. Institutions and private individuals sent donations, street parties sent profits and surplus money raised, and further cash was raised by a house-to-house collection and a flag day. By the spring of 1978 £16 million had been raised with more money to come. This means that an annual sum of £1 million a year can be devoted to youth projects

The Queen, The Prince of Wales and The Duke of Edinburgh arriving at St Paul's Cathedral for the Silver Jubilee service. They are led by the Lord Chamberlain, Lord Maclean, and followed by the Master of the Horse, the Duke of Beaufort.

The Prince of Wales at The Queen's Birthday Parade.

outlined by the Prince for a considerable number of years to come. Prince Charles and other members of the Royal Family attended many of the fund-raising events and the Prince chaired regular progress meetings. Organizers of the Appeal noted how much his self-confidence had grown and that he now made his own decisions rather than referring to his father for advice. Needless to say a lot of people thought Prince Charles was running the whole Jubilee and continually wrote asking him to come to Jubilee events.

As part of the celebrations, Prince Charles appeared on the television programme *Nationwide* and, to the consternation of the BBC, suggested that youngsters write to him about Silver Jubilee projects. *Nationwide* normally gets a thousand letters a day but with ten to twelve million people tuned in to watch the Prince, they feared a deluge. A spokesman for the programme consoled himself with the thought 'Luckily we can pass them to the Prince's staff to deal with.'

The Royal Family on the balcony of Buckingham Palace on Jubilee Day. *Left to right:* The Prince of Wales, Prince Edward, Princess Anne, Lord Mountbatten, The Queen, Prince Philip, Princess Margaret, Prince Andrew and The Queen Mother.

On 6 June he watched the Queen light the first of a chain of 102 bonfires that spread across Britain. After watching the lighting of a bonfire in New Zealand by Sir Edmund Hillary on a giant screen, the Prince's attention was caught by an ox which had been roasting with due ceremony throughout the proceedings. He turned to spectators near him and declared an interest in having a taste of it.

The following day, as a personal ADC to the Queen, Prince Charles rode behind the Gold State Coach to St. Paul's Cathedral. It was not an uneventful ride as he admitted later:

'I forgot we were due to stop at Temple Bar and was mesmerised by the wheels of the coach and trying to keep the right distance, but suddenly the coach stopped and I nearly fell off.'

His problems were, however, not yet over for when he dismounted at St. Pauls, the block was placed under the horse, so that the Prince missed it and nearly tumbled to the ground. He also fell foul of television cameras which zoomed in on the Prince at Temple Bar to catch what appeared to be an uncontrolled yawn. The explanation was that Prince Charles found it difficult to keep his bearskin on. 'I was moving my chin to keep the strap adjusted' he explained.

An alarming hereditary trait was revealed in the Daily Mirror in Jubilee week under the front page headline 'OOPS CHARLES! There's a patch in your thatch'. When he was twenty-eight, a bald spot 'the size of an egg' had been spotted. The lack of hair became apparent at a polo match at Cirencester when Prince Charles removed his polo helmet and failed to comb his hair to disguise the lacuna. It did not create anything like the panic and horror that had greeted the news that Prince Philip was thinning out in the late fifties.

At the end of a week that saw fireworks and an R.A.F. flypast and vast crowds, shouting 'We Want The Queen', Prince Charles was hailed as 'the epitome of martial, formal dignity' in the Sunday Express. The paper spoke of an 'almost self-mocking humility that is remarkable in the face of the deference and adulation with which he has always been surrounded.' Further accolades came in the world of polo, where it had long been thought that Prince Charles would be a better rider than his father but not as good a player for the reason that he spared his mount. However his Australian coach, Sinclair Hill said:

'He is fearless, has great positional sense and a technique that is almost without fault. I am confident that within two years I can turn him into a six handicap player (at the moment, he's a two) and that he will be captain of the England team.'

The Prince of Wales dressed as an Indian Chief in Canada in 1977.

In June Prince Charles visited a West Indian youth club, in South London and walked into the middle of a group of militant whites demonstrating against blacks and police. His message to them was to stop demonstrating and come together and talk about it. Buckingham Palace later commented that he had intervened in 'a potentially ugly situation'.

His action, which disturbed the police, was an indication of his intention to become more closely involved with political issues, an area traditionally avoided by the Royal Family. He has a good way with people as Harold Evans, Editor of the *Sunday Times* confirmed on the radio programme, Any Questions: 'He's got a marvellous way of asking questions and keeping a polite smile on his face'.

Jubilee Year ended with a family gathering for the christening of Princess Anne's son, who had been born on 15 November. Prince

Prince Charles dancing a samba in Rio de Janeiro at a party given by the Mayor during the Prince's eight-day goodwill visit to Brazil in 1978.

Charles, who was in Yorkshire at the time of the birth, was one of Master Peter Phillips's sponsors. In the Spring of 1978, Prince Charles visited Scotland. He had been invited to become a Freeman of the City of Edinburgh and had accepted, but the twenty-one Labour members of the City Council voted against him and the Freedom was withheld. One Labour Councillor stated: 'I would have thought that after the Silver Jubilee we had indulged in sufficient forelock touching to last us for ever'. Prince Charles spent the day in Glasgow.

In March he visited Brazil and Venezuela. In Rio he joined in a riotous samba to the cheers of one thousand guests. Back in England he underwent a ten day parachute course. On one jump he had to twist round to free his rigging but ended by making a perfect landing. 'My knees were knocking as I stood at the door,' said Prince Charles. 'The old adrenalin gets going when you're up there.'

Princess Kristine, Prince Charles
Bernadotte, Queen Silvia of Sweden,
King Carl Gustaf of Sweden, Queen
Margrethe of Denmark, Prince Charles,
(the late) Princess Georg of Denmark,
Prince Georg of Denmark, Princess
Ragnhild of Norway and Mr E.
Lorentzen, her husband, in the front
row for a gala in Oslo for King Olav's
75th birthday.

The Prince of Wales with the Crown
Prince of Iran and Queen Elizabeth The
Queen Mother at Royal Ascot in 1978.

Right:
The Prince of Wales and the Queen
Mother walking in the Garter
procession in June 1978.

The Prince of Wales and the Crown Prince of Iran in the Queen's carriage, arriving at Royal Ascot in June 1978.

There was an ugly incident when Prince Charles visited Newcastle upon Tyne. A man threw a lemonade bottle at his car shattering the window. Fortunately for him, the man was arrested before the crowd could do him much harm. One woman said: 'I was so furious I pulled the man's beard. I've still got some hair in my fingernails'. He attended the State Funeral of Sir Robert Menzies in Australia and that of President Jomo Kenyatta in Kenya. On the latter occasion he found himself seated three places away from Idi Amin, then President of Uganda. However, he avoided shaking Amin by the hand. In October he paid a five day visit to Yugoslavia.

Attention focussed on the Prince again in November when he reached his thirtieth birthday. He celebrated the occasion with a family dinner at Buckingham Palace and a dance for 350 guests. Earlier that evening he turned on the first Regent Street Christmas lights for seven years. He took a brief shooting holiday in Granada as a guest of the Duke and Duchess of Wellington, whose daughter Jane Wellesley was also present. Early in 1979 he repeated a successful skiing holiday in Klosters.

Since early in 1978, the Prince had no immediate project. He had left the Navy and completed the Jubilee appeal and therefore decided to

The Prince of Wales at the controls of a
Hawk trainer in November 1978.

devote some time to acquainting himself with 'the whole spectrum of
life in this country, with the world of industry, engineering, finance,
agriculture and government.'. He was to associate himself particularly
with the NEDC. Since then he has visited many factories, the Houses of
Parliament, 10 Downing Street, Lloyd's of London, and other such
institutions. Partly because of this, he has occasionally spoken his
mind, creating something of a stir. He became involved in religious
controversy when he condemned the church's preoccupation with
doctrinal matters, which, in his view, causes needless distress. He was
speaking at the time when Pope Paul VI had forbidden his cousin,
Prince Michael to wed in a Catholic marriage ceremony. In the Spring
of 1979 he attacked management executives, blaming them for many of

The Prince of Wales (Great Master) and Earl Mountbatten of Burma (Knight Grand Cross) at the installation ceremony of the Order of the Bath in May 1978.

Britain's industrial problems. This earned him praise from union leaders and rebukes from employers. In the summer he addressed the Trade Union Congress and urged the delegates to 'knock the stuffing' out of Britain's overseas competitors.

In April 1979 he flew to Hong Kong, the first stop of a six week tour of the Far East, Australia and Canada.

On 19 May Prince Charles visited Broadlands, the home of his great-uncle, Lord Mountbatten, and officially opened the house to tourists. He looked forward to returning there in October for a big celebration, the wedding of Norton Knatchbull, Lord Mountbatten's grandson, to Penelope Eastwood. Prince Charles had agreed to be best man.

Prince Charles left for a private fishing holiday in Iceland with Lord and Lady Tryon, while his great-uncle went to Ireland for his annual holiday at Classiebawn Castle. On August Bank Holiday Monday Lord Mountbatten and some of his family left for a few hours of fishing. Scarcely had they left the harbour when their boat was blown up by an IRA bomb. Lord Mountbatten and his grandson, Nicholas, were killed. So was a seventeen year old boatman, Paul Maxwell. Lord and Lady Brabourne and their other son, Timothy, were badly injured. Lord Brabourne's mother died the following day as a result of her injuries. On the same day eighteen soldiers were killed at Warrenpoint, County Down, and several more badly injured.

For Prince Charles this was an acutely personal tragedy. Lord Mountbatten was a great favourite of his and both clearly enjoyed each other's company enormously. On a wreath at his funeral, Prince Charles put the message: 'To my H.G.F. and G.U. from his loving and devoted H.G.S. and G.N.' Prince Charles did not explain the private code, but it was interpreted as an indication that Prince Charles had

'They that go down in ships . .' The Royal Family listen as the Prince of Wales reads the lesson at Lord Mountbatten's funeral in Westminster Abbey on 5 September 1979.

The Prince of Wales with Lord Mountbatten and the Duke of Edinburgh at a polo match at Smith's Lawn.

adopted Lord Mountbatten as his honorary grandfather. Lady Brabourne was a godmother to Prince Charles and he in turn was godfather to the twins, Nicholas and Timothy. As though this were not enough, sixteen of the eighteen men killed at Warrenpoint were from the Parachute Regiment of which Prince Charles is Colonel-in-Chief.

On hearing the news Prince Charles flew back immediately from Iceland. With Prince Philip, he was present at Eastleigh, Hants, as the Mountbatten family coffins were flown home. And Prince Charles, in Naval uniform, followed the coffin of Lord Mountbatten to the ceremonial funeral in Westminster Abbey. In a controlled voice, he read the lesson: 'They that go down in ships and occupy their business in great waters . . .' He had steeled himself to the task and fulfilled himself with supreme dignity, the respect of a Naval officer to an Admiral of the Fleet. Prince Charles travelled with the other mourners to Romsey Abbey for the interment. That night he stayed at Broadlands and is said to have taken a solitary walk, one he had often shared with his murdered great-uncle. The next day he and his father attended the simple burial of his godson, 'Nicky', and Doreen Lady Brabourne in a country churchyard at Mersham, Kent. At the end of September he read the lesson at a memorial service for the sixteen members of the Parachute Regiment and spent forty-five minutes with relatives afterwards. He shared with them his grief at his own bereavements.

In October Prince Charles fulfilled the role of best man to Norton Knatchbull, now Lord Romsey, at a service described by the Bishop of Winchester as a mixture of 'grief and joy, dismay and hope'. In December there was a memorial service for the victims. Prince Charles gave the address: 'What on earth was the point of such mindless cruelty?' he asked. And of Lord Mountbatten he said, 'I adored him and miss him so dreadfully now.' It was a sad note on which to enter the 1980s.

The Prince of Wales skiing at Klosters.

The Prince of Wales at the Peterborough Royal Show, July 1978.

144

The Bridal Path

When Prince Charles was in Canada in 1977, he was asked whether or not there was any truth in the story that he was about to name Princess Marie-Astrid of Luxembourg as his bride. He replied 'Oh! You don't believe all that stuff do you? It goes to show that you journalists are all romantics at heart!'

Over the years there have been two indications of what Prince Charles thought about marriage. The first came in a television interview in 1969, and has often been quoted. He was asked by Brian Connell about 'the lady the Prince should marry'. He replied that it was an awfully difficult question since, because of his position, the person whom he married would one day become Queen:

'You have got to choose somebody very carefully who could fulfil this particular role because people like you, perhaps, would expect quite a lot from somebody like that and it has got to be somebody pretty special.'

He enlarged on this theme five years later in a conversation with Kenneth Harris, who put it to him that it was unlikely that he would marry someone who was neither of royal lineage nor an aristocrat:

Kenneth Harris interviewing Prince Charles for the Observer in 1974.

'There's no essential reason why I shouldn't. I'd be perfectly free to. What would make it unlikely would be accidental, not essential. Whatever your place in life, when you marry you're forming a partnership which you hope will last, say, fifty years – I certainly hope so, because, as I told you, I've been brought up in a close-knit happy family and family life means more to me than anything else. So I'd want to marry someone who had interests which I understood and could share. Then look at it from the woman's point of view. A woman not only marries a man; she marries into a way of life in which she's got a contribution to make. She's got to have some knowledge of it, some sense of it, or she wouldn't have a clue about whether she's going to like it and if she didn't have a clue it would be risky for her, wouldn't it? If I'm deciding on whom I want to live with for fifty years – well, that's the last decision in which I would want my head to be ruled entirely by my heart. It's nothing to do with class; it's to do with compatibility. There are as many cases of marriages turning out unsatisfactorily because a man married "above" himself as there are when he married "below". Marriage isn't an "up" or "down" issue, anyway: it's a side-by-side one.'

These statements showed that Prince Charles was unlikely to precipitate himself into the kind of situation that the Duke of Windsor found himself in, though it is by no means unusual for members of the Royal Family to be more attracted to married people than to single ones. It appears that when confronted by royalty, married men and women tend to act with greater maturity. Theoretically the marriage question does not exist, and they either accept the Prince or reject him according to whether or not they like him personally. Princess Margaret, Prince William of Gloucester and Prince Michael of Kent have all experienced this. In the case of Prince William, Zsuzui Starkloff could not have been more enchanting. Prince William liked her for her beauty, intelligence and her conversation. Sadly it was impossible for them to marry because on paper everything was wrong. Apart from her rather un-royal name, she was a Hungarian divorcee, twice married, five years older than Prince William and with a teenage daughter living in New York. She summed up the attitude of princes and young girls by saying (of Prince William):

'The women they're trying to pair him off with at Buckingham Palace may be eligible because of their backgrounds. But they're all little girls. he's too much of a man for all that.'

Sir Oswald Mosley attacked the English ruling class at the time of the abdication of Edward VIII for 'stiff absurdity . . . when they rejected any form of marriage with an American of beauty, charm and character which would have been a link between two divergent outlooks in different civilisations'. Sir Oswald, viewing it from a political rather than from a religious or moral standpoint, thought that 'an honourable and natural alliance' between Edward VIII and Mrs Simpson would have been better than the humiliating way in which Great Britain later became 'a circling satellite of the American system.'

Speculation as to who the future Princess of Wales might be first began to arise in 1966. Dermot Morrah, examining all aspects of Prince Charles's development, began to enquire discreetly when Prince Charles's eye was first caught by the fairer sex. Evidently the Prince was unmoved by glamorous Mexican ladies presented to him on his homeward journey from Timbertop in July that year but on the other hand no less a person than the Queen told Morrah that at a Christmas party the following December she had been much amused by the dexterity with which her son homed in on the prettiest dancing partners. Dermot Morrah made his conclusions in language which says as much for his own wily sense of humour as it does for the direction of the Prince's proclivities:

'The inference seems to be that he has now established preferences in female loveliness and that his taste runs rather to the rosebuds of England than to the tiger lilies of the tropic south.'

Early, less well-informed suggestions of romance included an East Anglian neighbour, Rosaleen Bagge, daughter of Colonel Sir John Bagge, and just a year older than the Prince. She wrote to him a few times in Australia but underwent the embarrassment of having the correspondence discovered by journalists. The Bagge family suffered on one occasion a freezing stare from the Royal parents and nothing more came of the acquaintance. Ray Bellisario, the photographer, is proud to be dubbed 'a royal pain in the neck'. His professed view that he has 'republican attitudes towards people who regard themselves as rulers over others as of birthright' has not prevented him from selecting the Royal Family as his photographic targets and therefore a major source of his livelihood. He succeeded in obtaining a photograph of Prince Charles at a polo match at Cowdry Park with his distant cousin Princess Margarita of Rumania, but was even more delighted to catch on film an episode, which the press, ever eager for hints of royal romance, regarded as quite a scoop. In Malta in 1969 Sibella Dorman actually rubbed suntan lotion into the Prince of Wales's back and then the Prince rubbed suntan lotion into hers. This surely was it!

Royal Ascot, polo at Smith's Lawn and theatre-parties are the occasions on which potential future brides tend to be submitted to the scrutiny of the world. An early candidate was Lucia Santa Cruz, daughter of the Chilean Ambassador. Prince Charles had met her at Cambridge when she was helping Lord Butler with research for his memoirs. She was much in his company in 1970 and was not only a guest at Balmoral in September 1972 but accompanied him to the Festival Hall in the early months of 1973. Since then she has married.

In November 1970 came dramatic news of another female figure in the life of Prince Charles. In a party of four he escorted Bettina Lindsay to the theatre to see *The Secretary Bird* and the following night took her to the Albert Hall for a concert. Since she had been in the Royal Party at

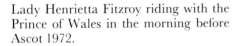

Lady Henrietta Fitzroy riding with the Prince of Wales in the morning before Ascot 1972.

Ascot the previous June, she was at once listed as a potential bride. The daughter of a Conservative Minister, Lord Balniel, Bettina had met the Prince at a dance given by the Marquess of Salisbury. Since then, according to the more flighty French press *'La Charme de Bettina a séduit la famille royale'*. It all seemed very suitable, thought the French, since the Crawford family had connexions with the Ogilvys and the Cavendishes, and readers were exhorted not to neglect the high significant point that Prince Charles's great-grandmother had been a *Cavendish*-Bentinck! It all depended, of course, on whether or not Prince Charles had actually held her hand during the play or not.

1971 produced no engagement with Bettina – she is now Mrs Peter Drummond-Hay – but by now there was a new candidate on the scene, widely photographed and frequently mis-named in the press, who danced with Prince Charles at a ball at Belvoir Castle, Leicestershire. His partner was his host's daughter, Lady Charlotte Manners. Disappointed at having nothing more definite to play with, *France Dimanche* began to predict his secret marriage to a French Catholic pop-star.

In March 1972, 'an attractive blonde in black slacks and cream tail-out shirt' appeared at Prince Charles's side at a polo match, when he was on leave from the Navy. She was later identified as Georgiana Russell, daughter of the British Ambassador in Brazil. She was presently replaced by the most long-standing and long-suffering candidate, Lady Jane Wellesley, daughter of the Duke of Wellington. However it was noted in 1973 that Georgiana was 'expected in the Caribbean where the Prince's ship had docked'.

Lady Jane, born in 1951, attended the Royal Tournament when Prince Charles took the salute in the Summer of 1972. the Prince was a guest at the Wellingtons' Granada estate in the autumn of 1972 and 1973. In September 1973 the press, excited at the prospect of Princess Anne's forthcoming nuptials, pursued Prince Charles everywhere. They photographed a girl called Rosie Clifton, coming off a train with Prince Michael of Kent, and swiftly linked her name with Prince Charles. When he flew back to his ship from Aberdeen Airport, he grinned at pressmen and said, 'By the way, gentlemen, I am not engaged. I hope you get that clear. There seem to be hundreds of you wherever I go.'

Prince Charles dancing with Lady Charlotte Manners at Belvoir in April 1971.

Lady Jane Wellesley at the wheel of her car in the Spring of 1974.

The Prince of Wales in Spain with Lady Jane Wellesley in 1973.

Miss Laura Jo Watkins in June 1974.

It made no difference when Buckingham Palace shrugged off the idea of marriage as 'pure speculation'. Credibility had been severely tested when a week or so before Princess Anne announced her engagement, the Press Officer of the time, Robin Ludlow, had instructed Fleet Street editors to leave the Princess alone as there was no truth in the story of a romance. He had not aimed to deceive the editors, genuinely believing what he said, but when royal love burgeoned into marriage, he felt obliged to resign.

During the 1973 Spanish holiday, far-fetched reports announced that Lady Jane had 'hugged and kissed the Prince during a shooting party'. As a result of this, the Old Bond Street Art Gallery where she worked was besieged and Lady Jane herself had to say 'There's no romance. We are just very good friends. It is nonsense what has been said by the Press.' Clearly she was disbelieved for after Christmas, despite a petrol crisis, 10,000 people headed to Sandringham to see her leave church with the Prince. Roads were jammed and traffic was affected as far back as the Midlands. The rumours reached inflated proportions when it was announced in 1974 that the Queen would attend the Game Fair at Stratfield Saye, the home of the Duke of Wellington the following July. Even the seemingly limitless patience of the Duke became strained, especially since the Prince of Wales was to be abroad at the time and would not be attending the fair. An indiscreet friend of Nicholas Soames (who had served occasionally as Prince Charles's equerry) went to dinner with Prince Charles the following summer and talked rather freely afterwards. The Prince was quoted as saying 'Jane is a jolly nice girl and I really pity her about the publicity.'

In June 1974, an American Roman Catholic appeared in London, and sat in the Gallery of the House of Lords to hear Prince Charles make his maiden speech. She was Laura Jo Watkins, the daughter of an American Rear-Admiral and had met Prince Charles in San Diego when his ship had come in a few months earlier. The press men were very direct in their approach to her. They passed her a note from the press gallery asking if she was 'the girl'. She smiled broadly, nodding confirmation. Laura Jo, a glamorous blonde, aged twenty, wore a pale yellow sleeved sweater, and an intriguing double-pearl ring on her engagement finger. It had no significance and she soon got fed up with the attendant publicity and returned to the States, where she was studying to be a legal secretary.

In the Autumn of 1974 Prince Charles told reporters in Melbourne that, contrary to what the English press thought, there was no special girl in his life. Perhaps for this reason the French scandal press had to invent a story that Prince Charles had donned a false beard (their art department swiftly applied the necessary shadow to his features) and had visited Lady Jane in her Fulham residence. This tryst would have remained a secret, said the paper, but for a sixty-year old lady living opposite who 'did not keep her tongue in her pocket'. In 1975 *The Times* revealed that *Hola*, a Spanish magazine which devotes much of its time to uniting and separating members of Royal Houses, had selected Princess Donata of Mecklenburg-Schwerin as the bride-to-be. Unfortunately she descended from the Duke of Cumberland and Prince Henry of Prussia, who were both on the German side in the First World War and had had their Garter banners removed from St. George's Chapel in 1915. This report in *The Times* provoked an unwelcome batch of sometimes unprintable letters, espousing the lady's cause. None were published.

1975 produced Penelope Eastwood, the daughter of a retired Major living in Majorca. She was occasionally seen in Prince Charles's company but a simple explanation for this may have been that she was the girl friend of Lord Romsey, then Norton Knatchbull, Lord Mountbatten's grandson. Penelope Eastwood was with the Royal Party for a polo match at Windsor in July 1975. Now she is Lady Romsey. Also present at polo was another lady, whose love-life received wide coverage in the 1970s. She was Princess Elizabeth of Yugoslavia, another guest of Lord Mountbatten and a one-time girl friend of actor, Richard Burton. At Cowdray Park she stood guard while Prince Charles changed his shirt at a polo match, quite a normal thing for a cousin to do. Prince Charles responded to the headlines that popped up with monotonous regularity with the healthy attitude:

'I almost felt I had better espouse myelf at once so as not to disappoint so many people.'

Miss Penelope Eastwood, now Lady Romsey, in March 1977.

The Prince of Wales driving down the Long Walk with Davina Sheffield.

Miss Davina Sheffield by Patrick Lichfield.

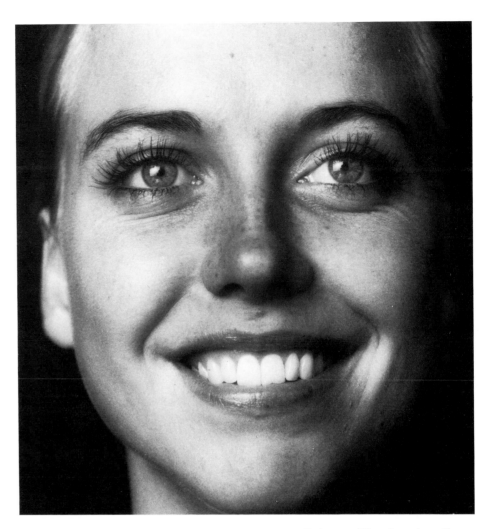

Davina Sheffield was introduced to Prince Charles by Jane Wellesley. She spent the August Bank Holiday week-end of 1974 with the Royal Family at Balmoral and turned the heads of a crowd of 4,000 when she attended morning service at Crathie Church. She then disappeared from the Royal scene until 1976. In the meantime she spent six weeks looking after sixty orphaned boys in Saigon and suffered the tragedy of her mother being murdered by youths at her Oxfordshire home. Davina succeeded in getting the journalists very excited. A former boyfriend, who said he had been unofficially engaged to her was quoted, or possibly misquoted, as saying:

'I think Prince Charles is a very impressive man and I am sure they will be very happy. I think she will make an extremely good Queen and a magnificent wife.'

Prince Charles was said to have comforted her after her mother's death, and when he was at Dartmouth they were spotted surfing together at 'a secluded Devon resort'. His sudden announcement in the Autumn of 1976 that he was leaving the Navy fanned the flames of journalistic ardour. A certain editor who likes to be prepared for royal engagements drew up an elaborate Sheffield family tree, which proved that Davina descended from the Earl of Mulgrave, whom Dryden called 'a most indifferent poet' and from the Buckinghams of Buckingham House, now Palace. Thus she was clearly pre-destined to live there. In addition to this, she was born on St David's Day 1951, a more than appropriate day for a future Princess of Wales. Sadly for the Press, the story of the romance was discovered some time after the Prince and Davina had stopped seeing each other.

The Prince of Wales enjoyed teasing the press. When journalists came on board his ship once he put up a picture of a blonde in his cabin to set their typewriters clicking. In 1977 the presence of an unidentified blonde was detected at his camp in Kenya. When Prince Charles left the airport at the end of his stay, he handed the *Daily Mirror* reporter a stuffed pigeon with some blonde human hair glued on its head, saying 'There's your mystery bird' and then departed before the Mirror man had time to utter 'That hair is real. The question is – where did it come from?'

Silver Jubilee Year pressed the claims of Princess Marie-Astrid of Luxembourg, who had become hot favourite after the Queen's State Visit to the Grand Duchy in the autumn of 1976. Her major disadvantage was that she was a Roman Catholic. Royalty can do no right in romance, it seems – even Princess Marie-Astrid's non-attendance of a May Ball at Cambridge, at which, incidentally, the Prince of Wales was not expected, was considered significant! The *Daily Express* nevertheless created a major journalistic blunder by covering the front page of 17 June 1977 with the headline 'CHARLES TO MARRY ASTRID'. The solution they produced to the Catholic problem was that sons would be Protestants and daughters Catholics. The announcement of an engagement was immediately denied by Buckingham Palace. The Catholic issue raised its head again in 1978 when Prince Michael of

Princess Marie-Astrid of Luxembourg.

Below: Lady Alexandra Hay.

Kent became engaged to Baroness Marie-Christine von Reibnitz, a Roman Catholic, who had been married to Tom Troubridge. When Prince Michael married her, he lost his rights of succession to the throne. Had he been permitted to retain his rights, he might have been a useful test case to facilitate a similar marriage by Prince Charles. Instead it would seem that a Catholic marriage for the Heir Apparent is impossible for many years to come.

In June 1977 Prince Charles escorted Lady Camilla Fane to Ascot and to the polo, but his most regular companion was the flame-haired Lady Sarah Spencer, elder sister of the bride. Lady Sarah was a New Year guest at Sandringham and accompanied the prince on a ski-ing visit to Klosters in January 1978. The *Daily Express* reporter quoted the Prince as saying 'It's all going very well' and then watched him enviously as they 'went inside the sloping-roofed chalet with a picture-postcard view.' In 1979, however, Lady Sarah became engaged to Neil McCorquodale, and they have since married.

The remaining months of 1978 produced no new candidates. Instead, the tipsters began to favour Lady Jane Wellesley, who reappeared on the royal scene, causing many to wonder if she had ever left it. As Prince Charles approached his 30th birthday, journalists wondered if perhaps he was going to surprise everyone with an announcement on the day. A rash statement years before – that he would like to marry at thirty – had haunted him and it was said that he looked harassed as 14 November approached. This was attributed to

The Prince of Wales with Lady Camilla Fane at Ascot in 1977. She is the daughter of the Earl of Westmorland, now Master of the Horse.

Lady Sarah Spencer, who has since married, in Klosters in January 1978.

The Prince of Wales at polo with Sabrina Guinness in 1979.

The Prince of Wales seized in public embrace by Jane Priest, a model, at Cottesloe Beach, Perth, Western Australia, in 1979.

two possibilities – either that he had a surprise up his sleeve or that he didn't. No announcement came and he survived the celebrations surrounded by numerous glamorous guests including Lady Jane, Lady Sarah Spencer, Lady Rose Nevill, Lady Camilla Fane, Princess Elizabeth of Yugoslavia, Nanette Newman, Susan George and Britt Ekland.

Nor did 1979 present anything substantial for the pressmen apart from two ridiculous incidents. The first occurred in Perth, when Jane Priest, a 25-year-old bikini-clad model and former mannequin of the year, primed a photographer and then chased the Prince during an early morning swim off Cottesloe Beach. Eager for a kiss, she pressed her form against his, an experience he might have enjoyed had the motives and the photographer not been so immediately apparent. The second incident, concerning Jane Ward, a 23 year old divorcee, was clearly something concocted by the press. Two newspapers went so far as to insert Prince Charles into photographs with Mrs Ward in an attempt to stir interest. Mrs Ward was asked to leave a polo match in which the Prince was playing and was quoted as saying: 'Enough harm has been done already. I may never see him again.'

During 1979 the names of the two Manners sisters, Elizabeth and Lucy, were mentioned here and there, but escaped publicity. The Prince stayed at Haddon, the home of Lord and Lady John Manners, when hunting in the Autumn. And following the Mountbatten tragedy, two of the Earl's grand daughters were added to the list, Lady Amanda Knatchbull, and her beautiful cousin, Edwina Hicks. The Prince was also seen in the company of Sabrina Guinness, one-time girlfriend of Mick Jagger.

Audrey Whiting, inveterate Royalty watcher, told her readers in 1977 that she knew who the bride would be. We must believe her since she was astute enough not to name the lady, thus preventing us from proving her wrong. Meanwhile Prince Charles himself has said: 'I've fallen in love with all sorts of girls and I fully intend on go on doing so'.

The Bride

Time rolled its ceaseless course, yet no bride emerged to take her place at the Prince of Wales's side. Throughout the last years of the 1970s nothing was easier than to start a rumour about the Prince's choice. Ever-romantic journalists were stirred time and again to action but in vain. Royal events occurred in merry succession, the Silver Jubilee, a grandson for the Queen, the Queen Mother's eightieth birthday, but still no wedding for the Heir to the Throne.

The fact that nothing happened was in itself interesting. What was the Prince hiding? Or was he perhaps hiding only the fact that he had nothing to hide from us? In 1980 the only candidate seemed to be Miss Anna Wallace, with whom he was sometimes seen in the hunting field, but she swiftly became engaged to somebody else.

Then on 17 September 1980, Nigel Dempster adopted a frank but confidential air of seriousness and devoted the whole of his *Daily Mail* Diary to the old question 'Has Charles found his future bride?' The new romance, he stressed, was in the very early stages and anything could happen to halt it, but Dempster was optimistic. The lady in question was Lady Diana Spencer, youngest daughter of Earl Spencer, of Althorp, Northamptonshire. Accompanying the article was a snatched picture of the possible bride, unrecognisable with her eyes down. That day the Press gathered at the Young England Kindergarten in St George's Square, Pimlico to photograph Lady Diana in her lunch

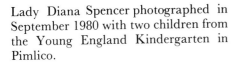

Lady Diana Spencer photographed in September 1980 with two children from the Young England Kindergarten in Pimlico.

break. She left her young charges and posed calmly and with dignity. The picture agencies hoped for the best, one insisting on world rights in colour at £180 for anything over half a page. The photographers did their best to make mischief, posing her with the light behind her printed skirt to give the nation an idea about her legs, swiftly pronounced prettier than those of television newsreader Angela Rippon. But despite this there was a feeling of sympathy towards this young lady and nothing was said against her.

Peace reigned for but a short time. When Princess Margaret celebrated her recent fiftieth birthday with a party at the Ritz on 4 November, Lady Diana sat next to Prince Charles with Jane Wellesley on his other side. Friends said he could not take his eyes off her, but no photographs were published to prove this.

Then on Sunday 9 November *The Sun* predicted a birthday engagement and the world went mad. The Young England Kindergarten was besieged, Lady Diana was photographed everywhere she went and journalists prepared profiles in the vain hope that their long vigil would end on Friday 14 November, the Prince's 32nd birthday.

Again, however, Nigel Dempster proved sound. While the Independent Television *News at Ten* devoted a major part of its programme to Lady Diana, he offered to wager a £1,000 personal bet with Sir Larry Lamb, Editor of *The Sun*, that nothing would happen that Friday. Each day he doubled this with confidence until £4000 was at stake. Asked on

Lady Diana caught by the press during the months of speculation. *Above left:* leaving the Ritz after Princess Margaret's birthday party in September. *Above right:* getting into the Mini Metro that Prince Charles gave her. *Below left:* leaving Lambourn after an early morning meeting with Prince Charles in January 1981. *Below centre:* leaving the Kindergarten. *Below right:* on her way to work.

the great day what he would do if he was proved wrong, he graciously joked that he would end it all. But 14 November came and went in silence and Dempster survived.

The night before the day in question Lady Diana suddenly disappeared, while Prince Charles went hunting. (They met during the weekend at Sandringham.) The press gathered hopefully outside Coleherne Court where Lady Diana lived. She proved, in the words of *The Times:* 'as scarce as last season's grouse'. One of Lady Diana's flatmates photographed the *mêlée* below the window, while the press consoled themselves by photographing Lady Diana's Renault receiving a parking ticket. Meanwhile a Buckingham Palace spokesman commented that she hoped that when the birthday was over, the press would let the matter rest.

But any lull was temporary. Lady Diana's flat remained besieged even when Prince Charles set off for a three week tour of India and Nepal. Fictitious stories were printed claiming that Lady Diana had had an assignation with the Prince on the Royal train, stories that were sternly jumped upon by the Queen's Press Secretary. Various journalists claimed to have secured interviews with Lady Diana, while the mischievous quietly circulated the rumour that the bride was to be Princess Marie-Astrid all along and that all this was an elaborate hoax to divert the hacks from the more complicated political and religious negotiations.

The next rumours were that the engagement might be announced on Christmas Day in the Queen's broadcast to the nation. The originators of this speculation failed to consider that the Queen records her talk some weeks in advance in order that it can be sent to all parts of the Commonwealth well in advance of the Christmas rush. The chance of maintaining secrecy would be nil.

The press held on to the story like hungry terriers. In January this year they besieged Sandringham to the extent that the Queen, unable to enjoy the normal privacy of her holiday, complained through her press secretary. 'The Queen has become increasingly angry about this, to put it bluntly,' he said. The death of Princess Alice, Countess of Athlone, at the age of 97 then put the court into mourning.

The Prince of Wales did not in fact propose until February. In an interview after the engagement was announced, he said that he had 'popped the question' just before Lady Diana departed for a long-planned, but secret, stay with her mother in Australia. She accepted almost at once. Lady Diana was to joke later about the problems of communicating during their separation. Australian voices on the telephone kept calling her mother's ranch claiming to be Buckingham Palace or the Prince himself. When Prince Charles announced himself, he too was disbelieved. He could not prove his identity over the telephone.

Lady Diana slipped quietly back into England in the middle of February after a twelve-day stay. And she was waiting in the Land Rover a few days later when Prince Charles's horse, Allibar, collapsed and died under him, while they were walking back from a work-out.

A few days later, on Tuesday 24 February at 11 a.m. the long awaited engagement was announced from Buckingham Palace. Months of speculation ended in euphoria on all sides. The brief announcement read:
'It is with the greatest pleasure that the Queen and the Duke of Edinburgh announce the betrothal of their beloved son, the Prince of Wales, to the Lady Diana Spencer, daughter of the Earl Spencer and the Honourable Mrs Shand Kydd.'

'The person, the merit and the family of Lady Diana Spencer are objects so valuable that they must necessarily have . . . caused many applications of this nature to Your Grace.' So wrote Philip, 4th Earl of Chesterfield, the 18th century statesman to Sarah, Duchess of Marlborough, requesting the hand in marriage of an earlier Lady Diana. By a curious coincidence of history, the great Sarah entertained a scheme to arrange a secret marriage between her favourite granddaughter, Lady Diana Spencer and the then Prince of Wales, remembered as 'Poor Fred'. She offered a dowry of £100,000, a considerable bait to the bankrupt Prince. But the Prime Minister, Sir Robert Walpole, discovered the plot and frustrated it at the last moment. Neither the Prince nor Lord Chesterfield were successful aspirants to Lady Diana's hand. In 1731 she married the 4th Duke of Bedford and died four years later at the age of twenty-five.

That Lady Diana Spencer was an ancestral aunt of her namesake seven generations later. Prince Charles's bride was born on 1 July 1961 and christened Diana Frances. That she is the younger sister of one of Prince Charles's previous girlfriends has a happy precedent in recent royal history. When he was twenty-five, Prince Henry, Duke of

Prince Charles on a skiing holiday with Lady Diana's elder sister Sarah in Klosters February 1978.

Lady Sarah Spencer with her parents, Earl Spencer and the Hon. Mrs Shand-Kydd at the wedding of Lady Jane to Mr Robert Fellowes in April 1978.

Gloucester was teased by his brother, the Prince of Wales, about a photograph of him with Lady Mary Montagu-Douglas-Scott. He looked at it for a while and riposted 'Right family, wrong girl'. In 1935 he married her elder sister, Lady Alice instead. She is now Princess Alice, Duchess of Gloucester.

Lady Diana was educated at Riddlesworth Hall, at West Heath, a public school near Sevenoaks, and in Switzerland. Recently she has worked as a kindergarten teacher. As her father has a home, Park Farm, near Sandringham, Lady Diana is thoroughly acquainted with the ways of royalty, but claims her first encounter with the Prince took place in November 1977. When her sister was much in his company, there was a dinner party at Althorp. Lady Sarah made a grand entrance on the arm of the Prince of Wales. This was the first night that Lady Diana had attended a grown-up dinner of this nature and her father was particularly impressed and delighted by the way she handled it. She has considerable natural charm and an ease of manner which will assist her greatly in the public life into which she now marries. In 1978 a new close link with the Court was forged when Lady Jane Spencer, her other sister, married Robert Fellowes, Assistant Private Secretary to the Queen since Silver Jubilee Year, and son of Sir William Fellowes, for many years Land Agent at Sandringham. Lady Diana was a bridesmaid.

Lady Jane and Lady Diana, the younger sisters, are more statuesque than Lady Sarah who, as one friend put it, 'you could blow away like a feather'. Lady Sarah is a god-daughter of the Queen Mother, Lady Jane, a fashion assistant at *Vogue* until her marriage, is a god-daughter

Left: The wedding of Mr Robert Fellowes to Lady Jane Spencer at the Guard's Chapel, London, in April 1978. Lady Diana (the bride's younger sister) was the senior bridesmaid.

Lord and Lady Fermoy in 1933.

Left: Lady Diana's parents, then Viscount and Viscountess Althorp at their wedding in Westminster Abbey in 1954, and Princess Margaret leaving the Abbey with Lord Fermoy, father of the bride.

Below: Miss Phyllis Sellick and Lady Fermoy, OBE, playing triangles in a 'Toy Symphony' at the Savoy Hotel in aid of the Musicians' Benevolent Fund in 1953. *Below right:* Dr Mary Woodall and Ruth, Lady Fermoy, looking at Henry Moore's *King and Queen* in the garden of the Guildhall, King's Lynn.

of the Duke of Kent, while their brother Viscount Althorp, born in 1964, is a godson of the Queen. (He is the second but only surviving son of Earl Spencer. His elder brother, John, died soon after birth on 12 January 1960.)

Nowhere will Lady Diana's wedding be more eagerly celebrated than at Clarence House, for both the bride's grandmothers and four of her great-aunts have been very close members of the Queen Mother's court. The Prince of Wales has always been very devoted to the Queen Mother, but he was also very close to his great-uncle, Lord Mountbatten. One of the late Earl's granddaughters, Lady Amanda Knatchbull, was known as 'the long stop' in the Royal Family when Prince Charles's possible marriage was discussed. This wedding is therefore very much a Windsor rather than a Mountbatten wedding.

Lady Diana's mother, Frances, was divorced from her father in 1969 and is now married to Peter Shand Kydd. They farm on the Isle of Seil, Argyll. Mrs Shand Kydd's mother is Ruth, Lady Fermoy, a Woman of the Bedchamber to the Queen Mother from 1960 (and an Extra Woman of the Bedchamber for four years before that). Ruth, Lady Fermoy is a quiet, dignified lady who is a keen and accomplished

musician. When the present author met her in 1979 and matters concerning the Royal Family were discussed, she was torn between being helpful and showing the discretion that her close intimacy with the Queen Mother demands. In the nicest possible way the latter won. She runs the King's Lynn Festival in Norfolk, which the Queen Mother supports and attends as Patron. She is a Dame Commander of the Royal Victorian Order and a Justice of the Peace in Norfolk.

Lady Diana's father, the 8th Earl Spencer, is known to his friends as Johnny. Born in 1924 and a godson to Queen Mary and the Duke of Windsor, he served in the Second World War in the Royal Scots Greys and was later ADC to the Governor of South Australia. He served as Equerry to King George VI from 1950 to 1952 and was often a guest at Balmoral, where with Prince Philip and others, he used to set off in pursuit of hares, grouse and snipe. (He appears as 'Althorp' in the late King's game book.) He was then ADC to the present Queen for a further two years. He is a Deputy Lieutenant of Northamptonshire and Chairman of the National Association of Boys' Clubs, whose President is the present Duke of Gloucester, as well as being a leading member of the Royal Jubilee Trusts.

In 1975 he succeeded to the Earldom of Spencer on the death of his father. His first marriage to Lady Diana's mother was dissolved, and in 1976 he married Raine, formerly Countess of Dartmouth, who is well known to the general public as a member of the Greater London

Barbara Cartland, the prolific novelist and step-grandmother of the bride.

Earl and Countess Spencer in London on the day of the announcement. Lady Spencer is the bride's stepmother.

Council and a society figure. Her mother is the famous and prolific romantic novelist, Barbara Cartland. The present Countess Spencer is famed for undertaking a morning 'toilette' almost in the style of the French courts of Versailles. Not by nature a country person, she greatly enjoys serving in the Althorp shop, when the house is open to the public. Amusement was caused at a Northamptonshire dinner table some years ago when the host, a lofty old Etonian, who had sat in silence throughout the first course, suddenly turned to her and enquired: 'What did you say your name was? Storm?' – 'No, Raine,' she replied. 'Ah! Yes,' he said in a downward dropping voice, 'I knew it had something to do with the weather'. The Spencers maintain a curious domestic arrangement in London. They live in the penthouse of the block in which the Earl of Dartmouth lives with his new wife. Lord Spencer was recently gravely ill, but celebrated his recovery with a service of thanksgiving in Northamptonshire in the autumn of 1979. This service was attended by many society figures and by the then Leader of the House of Commons, Mr Norman St John Stevas.

Lady Diana Spencer is a seventh cousin (once removed) to the Prince of Wales. She is a second cousin of the Duke of Abercorn, and both a fifth cousin and a second cousin (once removed) of the vanished Earl of Lucan. She is a seventh cousin (once removed) of the present Duke of Marlborough, who quarters the Spencer arms with those of Churchill, just as he hyphenates the name of Spencer with Churchill. Lady Diana is dynastically connected with the Dukes of Bedford, Grafton and Richmond. Georgiana, Duchess of Devonshire, in whose day Devonshire House in Piccadilly became 'the centre of a brilliant conspiracy of Whig patricians' and her sister, the Countess of Bessborough, another leader in Whig society, are dynastic aunts, while Maurice Baring, the poet and essayist, is a great-great-uncle. Above all Lady Diana descends four times over from King Charles II and once from King James II. She thus has six lines of descent from Mary, Queen of Scots. Curiously enough, Prince Charles himself descends from neither of the later Royal Stuarts, and so Lady Diana brings their blood back to the Royal Family.'

Charles II after a portrait by Sir Peter Lely.

The Spencers became rich from extensive sheep farming nearly 500 years ago. The descend from Sir John Spencer, of Wormleighton in Warwickshire, who bought Althorp in 1506 and who died on 14 April 1522. Knighted by King Henry VIII, he is reputed to have been a 'noble housekeeper, liberal to his poor neighbours, and bountiful to his tenants and servants'. Sir John claimed descent from Robert Despencer, William the Conqueror's steward, and from a branch of those Despencers who were the favourites of Edward II. The family fortunes were further augmented when his grandson, also Sir John Spencer, married the eldest daughter of Sir Thomas Kytson, known as 'Kytson the merchant', who owned land in Suffolk, and whose warehouses were discovered at his death to be filled with cloth of gold, satins, tapestry, velvets, furs and fustians of enormous value.

Sir John Spencer's son, the third Sir John of the family, was knighted in 1588 and died at the turn of that century. He married Mary, daughter of Sir Robert Catlin, the judge who presided at the trial of the Duke of Norfolk when he was charged with high treason for conspiring with Mary Queen of Scots to dethrone Elizabeth I. He was the father of Sir Robert Spencer, the fifth of the family to be knighted (in 1600). Sir Robert was Sheriff of Northamptonshire and an assiduous breeder of sheep. He was said to be the wealthiest man in England when James I succeeded to the throne. In July 1600 he was created 1st Baron Spencer of Wormleighton and the following September he was the principal ambassador representing 'the Sovereign's person' at the investiture of Frederick, Duke of Württemberg as a Knight of the Garter at Stuttgart Cathedral. The magnificent ceremonies and the feast that followed took five pages to describe in the annals of the Order of the Garter.

Lord Spencer married Margaret, daughter of Sir Francis Willoughby of Wollaton, Northants. After her death in 1597 he remained a widower, a fact to which Ben Jonson pays tribute in his lines:

> Who, since Thamyra did die
> Hath not brook'd a lady's eye,
> Nor allow'd about his place
> Any of the female race.

There are several versions of an exchange recorded between Lord Spencer and Thomas Howard, Earl of Arundel, which brought the Baron into prominence in 1621. The most famous is that during a debate on the Royal Prerogative, Howard said: 'My Lord, when these things were doing, your ancestors were keeping sheep.' To which Lord

James II by Sir Godfrey Kneller.

Spencer replied: 'When my ancestors were keeping sheep, Your Lordship's ancestors were plotting treason'. It appears, however, that the more likely version is that in a speech Lord Spencer referred to Norfolk and Surrey, Lord Arundel's beheaded ancestors, which provoked the jibe about the sheep. When Arundel refused to apologize, he was committed to the Tower.

Lord Spencer had four sons. His second son, the 2nd Baron Spencer of Wormleighton, married Penelope Wriothesley, daughter of the 3rd Earl of Southampton, whom the 1st Baron had keenly supported in domestic politics. Their son, Henry, was created Earl of Sunderland in 1643. Henry's wife was formerly Lady Dorothy Sidney, the inspiration of the poet, Edmund Waller, who called her 'Sacharissa'. The Spencers lived a happy and quiet life at Althorp until the outbreak of the Civil War when Henry enlisted in the Royal army and loaned the King £10,000. He was a keen supporter of the Crown, while not admiring its wearer. He wrote to his wife that he would rather be hanged than fight for Parliament. Charles I trusted him and sent him as envoy to Parliament with his friend, Falkland. A year later Henry and Falkland were killed side by side at the Battle of Newbury.

Robert Spencer, 2nd Earl of Sunderland, KG (1640–1702) was Henry's son. He was a rogue of few scruples, whose extraordinary career included being Ambassador to Paris, Cologne and Madrid. He was treacherous, profligate, rapacious and forever involved in intrigue. In 1679 he became Secretary of State and a member of the small circle that surrounded Charles II. He later supported James II, not neglecting to maintain close secret contact with William of Orange. In 1688 he declared himself a Papist, but he changed to the Anglican faith when he supported William. This was considered a matter of expediency at the time. He was Lord Chamberlain for a short spell in 1697. His career is best summarized in four lines from a contemporary lampoon:

A Proteus, ever acting in disguise;
A finished statesman, intricately wise;
A second Machiavel, who soar'd above
The little tyes of gratitude and love

Lord Sunderland's wife was Lady Anne Digby, a Lady of the Bedchamber to Queen Mary of Modena and to Queen Anne. She was as clever and versatile as her husband.

Their second son, Charles Spencer, 3rd Earl of Sunderland, KG (1674–1722) was a statesman and bibliophile. As crooked as his father, he was also violently assertive. Burnet noted that he treated Queen Anne rudely and 'chose to reflect in a very injurious manner upon all princes before her'. Nevertheless he held high office under Anne and her successor, George I, becoming Prime Minister in 1718, before being ruined by the South Sea Bubble. He married Lady Anne Churchill, daughter of the great Duke of Marlborough. This is where the family divides. The 4th Earl was succeeded as 5th Earl by his brother, who in turn became 3rd Duke of Marlborough. The younger brother, the Honourable John Spencer (1708–46) succeeded to Althorp and it is from him that the Earls Spencer descend. It is also at this point that the characters of the two families of Spencer and Spencer-Churchill diverge. The Spencers were artistic, charming and addicted to play. The Churchills were drawn to political and military life, and many have been melancholic; the tenure of Blenheim has weighed heavily on many a Duke and Duchess. The Spencers were fortunate in inheriting a considerable sum of money from Sarah, Duchess of Marlborough, and

Althorp in Northamptonshire, the ancestral home of the Spencers.

as a result they became connoisseurs. According to the historian, A. L. Rowse: 'Connoisseurship ran in their veins and they spent fortunes upon medals and antiquities, painting and sculpture – just what Sarah hated: that and gaming.' Sarah arranged a political alliance between John and Georgina, the daughter of her political friend against Walpole, Lord Carteret. The couple were happy, though they were out of favour at court. In 1734 King George II turned his back on them and all Queen Caroline could say was: 'I think, Mr Spencer, I have not seen you since you was a child.'

There were six Earls Spencers before Lady Diana's grandfather. Four of them were Knights of the Garter, but only the 1st, 2nd, 4th and 6th Earls are direct ancestors. John, 1st Earl Spencer (1734–83) was a collector of works of art, who built and furnished Spencer House in London. He was a Whig Member of Parliament for some years. In 1761 he was created Baron Spencer of Althorp and Viscount Spencer of Althorp, and in 1765 he was created Viscount Althorp and Earl Spencer. He married Georgiana Poyntz in a secret ceremony in his mother's dressing room at Althorp in December 1755. Although there were nearly 500 people in the house at the time of the ceremony, nobody knew about it until the following Saturday. The marriage was a happy one.

Their only son, George John, was the 2nd Earl Spencer, KG (1758–1834). He had a distinguished Whig career, was Lord Privy Seal in 1794, and First Lord of the Admiralty from 1794 to 1801, six years which have been described as 'the most stirring, the most glorious in our naval history, so that for him, more distinctly perhaps than for any other English administrator, may be claimed the title of organizer of victory.' Besides the great battles won during those years, it was under him that Nelson was singled out for independent command. He was Home Secretary under Charles James Fox from 1806 to 1807. After that he devoted himself to literary and scientific pursuits in Northampton-shire and rehabilitated the Althorp library. He married Lady Lavinia Bingham, daughter of the 1st Earl of Lucan, in 1781. She was very beautiful, intelligent and charming, one of the most prominent women in London society and a friend of numerous eminent, literary, naval and political men.

John Charles, the 3rd Earl Spencer (1782–1845), is not a direct ancestor of the bride, but her ancestral uncle. His career is perhaps the most distinguished of the Spencers. He declined the office of Prime Minister but was Chancellor of the Exchequer and Leader of the House of Commons until he succeeded his father in 1834, when he withdrew from politics and court life. But while in office, he was closely involved with the introduction and carrying of the Great Reform Bill. Greville wrote of him: 'He was the very model and type of an English gentle-man . . . Modest without diffidence, confident without vanity, ardently desiring the good of his country, without the slightest personal ambition . . . His friends followed this plain and simple man with enthusiastic devotion, and he possessed the faculty of disarming his political antagonists of all bitterness and animosity towards him.'

When the 3rd Earl died, he was succeeded by the next surviving brother, who was the fourth son of the 2nd Earl. Frederick, 4th Earl Spencer, KG (1798–1857) served in the Navy and then as a courtier. He was Equerry to the Duchess of Kent from 1840 to 1845, Lord Chamberlain from 1846 to 1848 and Lord Steward from 1854 to 1857. In 1830 he married his second cousin, Elizabeth Poyntz, who died in 1851. She was the mother of the 5th Earl. Then in 1854 he married Lord Alcester's sister, Adelaide Seymour, who died in 1877, his son by his second marriage was the 6th Earl, Lady Diana's great-grandfather.

John Poyntz Spencer, 5th Earl Spencer, KG (1835–1910) (known as the Red Earl) was a prominent Liberal, a keen sportsman and a close personal friend of the Prince of Wales. As early as 1864 the Prince pressed his claims to be a Knight of the Garter, but Lord Spencer was diffident. 'I am sure the Queen would not like your refusing and I am quite certain that I should not,' wrote the Prince. He was delighted when Lord Spencer, later an ardent home ruler, became Lord Lieutenant of Ireland in 1868. (He served until 1874 and again from 1882 to 1885.) The Prince paid him a highly successful visit in Dublin in 1868. Both in 1871 and 1885 Lord Spencer tried to have the Prince appointed a non-political Lord Lieutenant in his stead, but each time he failed. 'I feel inclined to throw up the sponge and retire to my plough in Northamptonshire,' he wrote sadly in May 1885. While in Ireland, Lord Spencer had a most unfortunate drama on his hands. This was a case of a popular skipper on board a small vessel who had joked that he had acquired some irons. The crew merrily agreed to try them out. Only the cabin boy was missing but they did not wait for him. When the boy came up from the hold he witnessed the Captain solemnly lopping off the heads of each member of the crew in turn. The boy escaped and the Captain was later declared insane and incarcerated in a criminal lunatic asylum. There he languished for twenty years, showing no signs of abnormality again, but surrounded by moronic beings who gave him little peace. Lord Spencer was moved to release him. The story has a sad end. The Captain was so excited at the prospect of freedom that he lost his self-control and attacked his warders. His reprieve was withdrawn.

Subsequently Lord Spencer was Lord President of the Council from 1880 to 1882 and again in 1886. His duties involved travelling to Osborne with Sir William Harcourt to discuss the Queen's Speech with

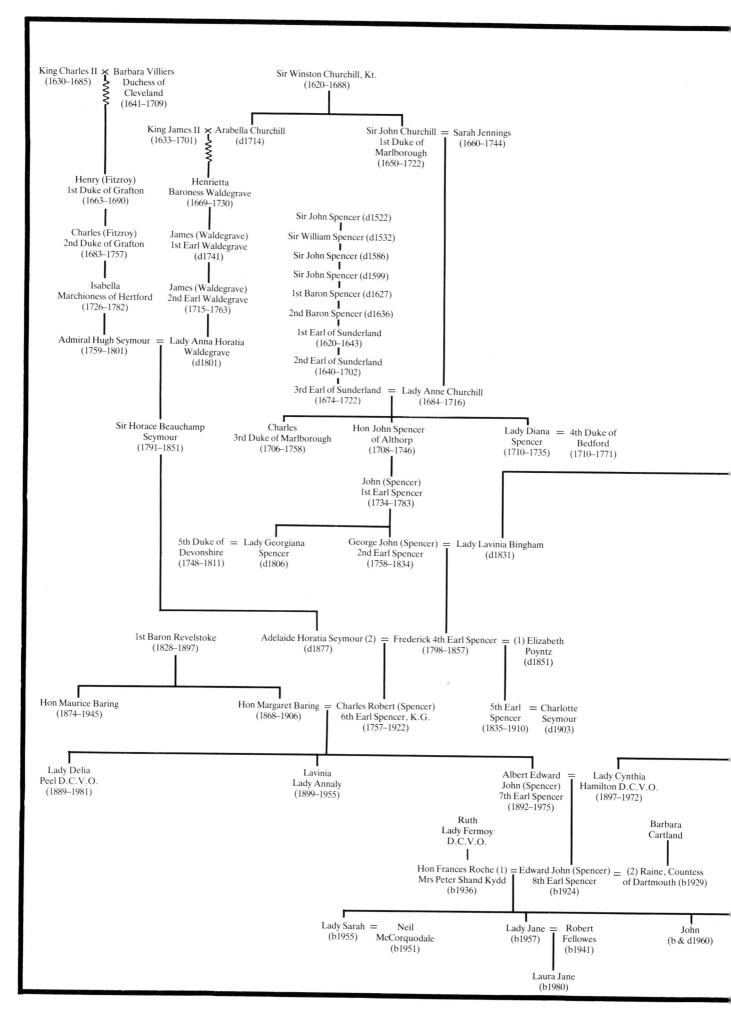

King Charles II ✕ Barbara Villiers
(1630–1685)   Duchess of
Cleveland
(1641–1709)

Sir Winston Churchill, Kt.
(1620–1688)

King James II ✕ Arabella Churchill
(1633–1701)   (d1714)

Sir John Churchill = Sarah Jennings
1st Duke of   (1660–1744)
Marlborough
(1650–1722)

Henry (Fitzroy)
1st Duke of Grafton
(1663–1690)

Henrietta
Baroness Waldegrave
(1669–1730)

Charles (Fitzroy)
2nd Duke of Grafton
(1683–1757)

James (Waldegrave)
1st Earl Waldegrave
(d1741)

Sir John Spencer (d1522)

Sir William Spencer (d1532)

Sir John Spencer (d1586)

Sir John Spencer (d1599)

1st Baron Spencer (d1627)

2nd Baron Spencer (d1636)

1st Earl of Sunderland
(1620–1643)

Isabella
Marchioness of Hertford
(1726–1782)

James (Waldegrave)
2nd Earl Waldegrave
(1715–1763)

2nd Earl of Sunderland
(1640–1702)

Admiral Hugh Seymour = Lady Anna Horatia
(1759–1801)   Waldegrave
(d1801)

3rd Earl of Sunderland = Lady Anne Churchill
(1674–1722)   (1684–1716)

Sir Horace Beauchamp
Seymour
(1791–1851)

Charles
3rd Duke of Marlborough
(1706–1758)

Hon John Spencer
of Althorp
(1708–1746)

Lady Diana = 4th Duke of
Spencer   Bedford
(1710–1735) (1710–1771)

John (Spencer)
1st Earl Spencer
(1734–1783)

5th Duke of = Lady Georgiana
Devonshire   Spencer
(1748–1811)   (d1806)

George John (Spencer) = Lady Lavinia Bingham
2nd Earl Spencer   (d1831)
(1758–1834)

1st Baron Revelstoke
(1828–1897)

Adelaide Horatia Seymour (2) = Frederick 4th Earl Spencer = (1) Elizabeth
(d1877)   (1798–1857)   Poyntz
(d1851)

Hon Maurice Baring
(1874–1945)

Hon Margaret Baring = Charles Robert (Spencer)
(1868–1906)   6th Earl Spencer, K.G.
(1757–1922)

5th Earl = Charlotte
Spencer   Seymour
(1835–1910) (d1903)

Lady Delia
Peel D.C.V.O.
(1889–1981)

Lavinia
Lady Annaly
(1899–1955)

Albert Edward =
John (Spencer)
7th Earl Spencer
(1892–1975)

Lady Cynthia
Hamilton D.C.V.O.
(1897–1972)

Ruth
Lady Fermoy
D.C.V.O.

Barbara
Cartland

Hon Frances Roche (1) = Edward John (Spencer) = (2) Raine, Countess
Mrs Peter Shand Kydd   8th Earl Spencer   of Dartmouth (b1929)
(b1936)   (b1924)

Lady Sarah = Neil
(b1955)   McCorquodale
(b1951)

Lady Jane = Robert
(b1957)   Fellowes
(b1941)

John
(b & d1960)

Laura Jane
(b1980)

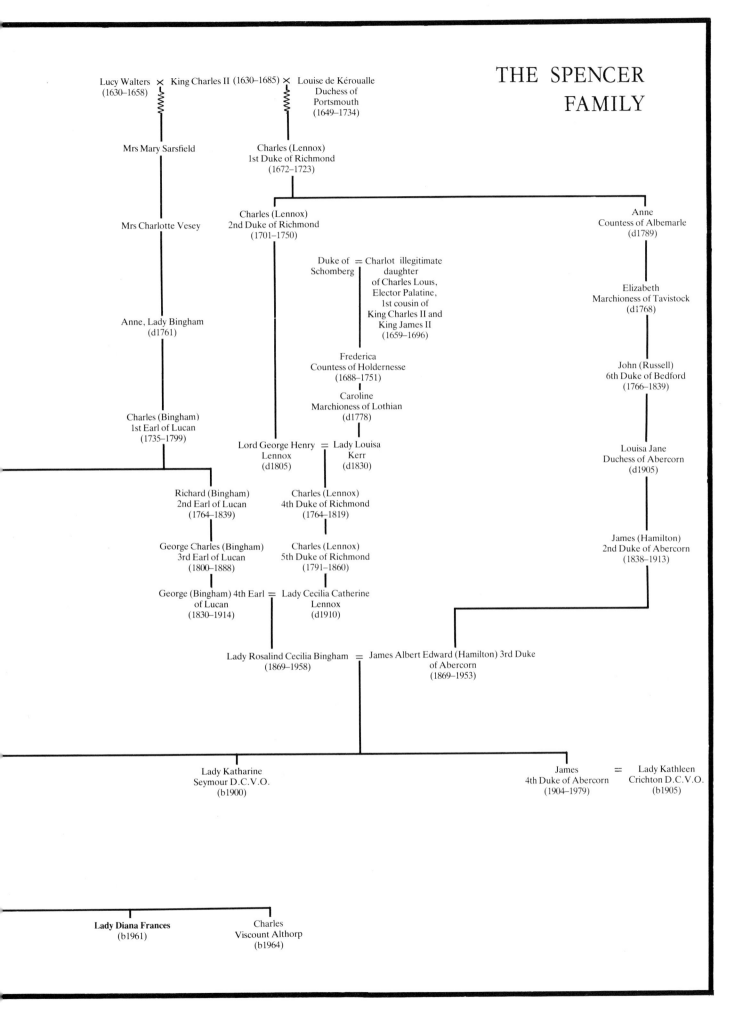

THE SPENCER
FAMILY

Lucy Walters ✕ King Charles II (1630–1685) ✕ Louise de Kéroualle
(1630–1658)   Duchess of
                                                     Portsmouth
                                                     (1649–1734)

Mrs Mary Sarsfield   Charles (Lennox)
                                1st Duke of Richmond
                                (1672–1723)

Mrs Charlotte Vesey   Charles (Lennox)   Anne
                           2nd Duke of Richmond   Countess of Albemarle
                           (1701–1750)   (d1789)

                                    Duke of = Charlot illegitimate   Elizabeth
                                    Schomberg   daughter   Marchioness of Tavistock
                                               of Charles Lous,   (d1768)
                                               Elector Palatine,
                                               1st cousin of
                                               King Charles II and
Anne, Lady Bingham   King James II
(d1761)   (1659–1696)

                                    Frederica   John (Russell)
                                    Countess of Holdernesse   6th Duke of Bedford
                                    (1688–1751)   (1766–1839)
                                    Caroline
                                    Marchioness of Lothian
                                    (d1778)

Charles (Bingham)   Lord George Henry = Lady Louisa   Louisa Jane
1st Earl of Lucan   Lennox   Kerr   Duchess of Abercorn
(1735–1799)   (d1805)   (d1830)   (d1905)

            Richard (Bingham)   Charles (Lennox)
            2nd Earl of Lucan   4th Duke of Richmond
            (1764–1839)   (1764–1819)

            George Charles (Bingham) Charles (Lennox)   James (Hamilton)
            3rd Earl of Lucan   5th Duke of Richmond   2nd Duke of Abercorn
            (1800–1888)   (1791–1860)   (1838–1913)

            George (Bingham) 4th Earl = Lady Cecilia Catherine
            of Lucan   Lennox
            (1830–1914)   (d1910)

            Lady Rosalind Cecilia Bingham = James Albert Edward (Hamilton) 3rd Duke
            (1869–1958)   of Abercorn
                                               (1869–1953)

            Lady Katharine   James   = Lady Kathleen
            Seymour D.C.V.O.   4th Duke of Abercorn   Crichton D.C.V.O.
            (b1900)   (1904–1979)   (b1905)

Lady Diana Frances   Charles
(b1961)   Viscount Althorp
                                (b1964)

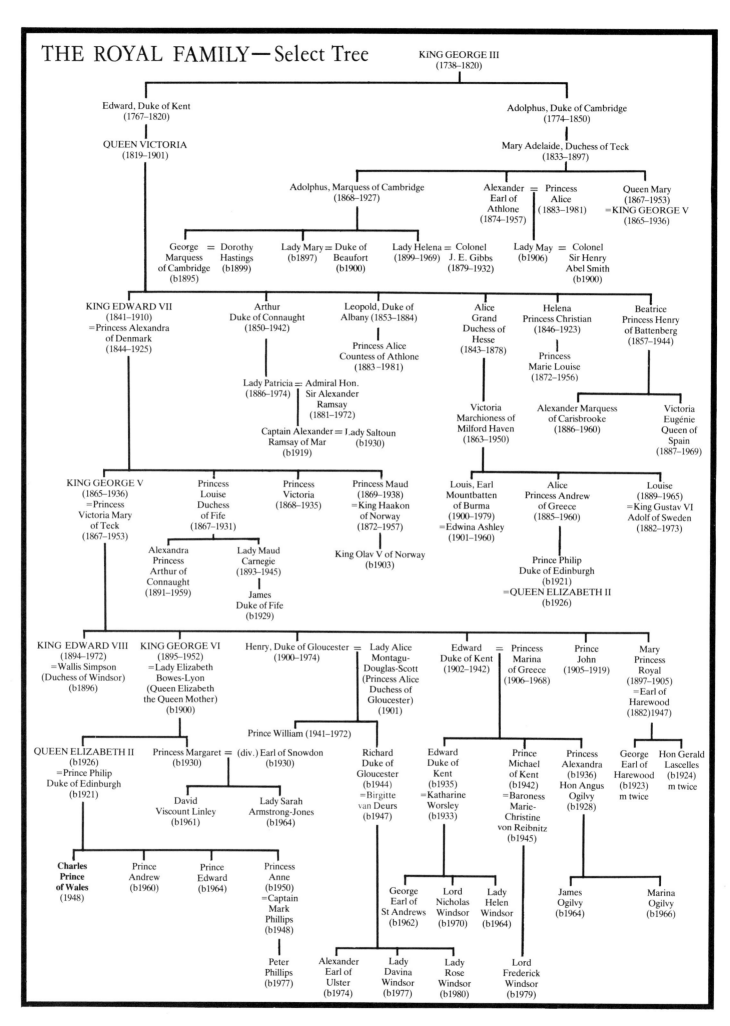

THE ROYAL FAMILY — Select Tree

KING GEORGE III (1738–1820)

Edward, Duke of Kent (1767–1820)

Adolphus, Duke of Cambridge (1774–1850)

QUEEN VICTORIA (1819–1901)

Mary Adelaide, Duchess of Teck (1833–1897)

Adolphus, Marquess of Cambridge (1868–1927)

Alexander Earl of Athlone (1874–1957) = Princess Alice (1883–1981)

Queen Mary (1867–1953) =KING GEORGE V (1865–1936)

George Marquess of Cambridge (b1895) = Dorothy Hastings (b1899)

Lady Mary (b1897) = Duke of Beaufort (b1900)

Lady Helena (1899–1969) = Colonel J. E. Gibbs (1879–1932)

Lady May (b1906) = Colonel Sir Henry Abel Smith (b1900)

KING EDWARD VII (1841–1910) =Princess Alexandra of Denmark (1844–1925)

Arthur Duke of Connaught (1850–1942)

Leopold, Duke of Albany (1853–1884)

Alice Grand Duchess of Hesse (1843–1878)

Helena Princess Christian (1846–1923)

Beatrice Princess Henry of Battenberg (1857–1944)

Princess Alice Countess of Athlone (1883–1981)

Princess Marie Louise (1872–1956)

Lady Patricia (1886–1974) = Admiral Hon. Sir Alexander Ramsay (1881–1972)

Victoria Marchioness of Milford Haven (1863–1950)

Alexander Marquess of Carisbrooke (1886–1960)

Victoria Eugénie Queen of Spain (1887–1969)

Captain Alexander Ramsay of Mar (b1919) = Lady Saltoun (b1930)

KING GEORGE V (1865–1936) =Princess Victoria Mary of Teck (1867–1953)

Princess Louise Duchess of Fife (1867–1931)

Princess Victoria (1868–1935)

Princess Maud (1869–1938) =King Haakon of Norway (1872–1957)

Louis, Earl Mountbatten of Burma (1900–1979) =Edwina Ashley (1901–1960)

Alice Princess Andrew of Greece (1885–1960)

Louise (1889–1965) =King Gustav VI Adolf of Sweden (1882–1973)

Alexandra Princess Arthur of Connaught (1891–1959)

Lady Maud Carnegie (1893–1945)

King Olav V of Norway (b1903)

Prince Philip Duke of Edinburgh (b1921) =QUEEN ELIZABETH II (b1926)

James Duke of Fife (b1929)

KING EDWARD VIII (1894–1972) =Wallis Simpson (Duchess of Windsor) (b1896)

KING GEORGE VI (1895–1952) =Lady Elizabeth Bowes-Lyon (Queen Elizabeth the Queen Mother) (b1900)

Henry, Duke of Gloucester (1900–1974) = Lady Alice Montagu-Douglas-Scott (Princess Alice Duchess of Gloucester) (1901)

Edward Duke of Kent (1902–1942) = Princess Marina of Greece (1906–1968)

Prince John (1905–1919)

Mary Princess Royal (1897–1905) =Earl of Harewood (1882)1947)

Prince William (1941–1972)

QUEEN ELIZABETH II (b1926) =Prince Philip Duke of Edinburgh (b1921)

Princess Margaret (b1930) = (div.) Earl of Snowdon (b1930)

Richard Duke of Gloucester (b1944) =Birgitte van Deurs (b1947)

Edward Duke of Kent (b1935) =Katharine Worsley (b1933)

Prince Michael of Kent (b1942) =Baroness Marie-Christine von Reibnitz (b1945)

Princess Alexandra (b1936) Hon Angus Ogilvy (b1928)

George Earl of Harewood (b1923) m twice

Hon Gerald Lascelles (b1924) m twice

David Viscount Linley (b1961)

Lady Sarah Armstrong-Jones (b1964)

Charles Prince of Wales (1948)

Prince Andrew (b1960)

Prince Edward (b1964)

Princess Anne (b1950) =Captain Mark Phillips (b1948)

George Earl of St Andrews (b1962)

Lord Nicholas Windsor (b1970)

Lady Helen Windsor (b1964)

James Ogilvy (b1964)

Marina Ogilvy (b1966)

Peter Phillips (b1977)

Alexander Earl of Ulster (b1974)

Lady Davina Windsor (b1977)

Lady Rose Windsor (b1980)

Lord Frederick Windsor (b1979)

her. On an occasion in 1881 there was an interminable row about it with the sole result, as Lord Esher noted, 'that Harcourt and Lord S. will miss their dinner.' Lord Spencer was then First Lord of the Admiralty from 1892 to 1895. When the Government resigned, Queen Victoria wrote to Empress Frederick that this was 'not such a source of satisfaction as it might have been for I am losing some people who cannot be replaced.' One was Lord Spencer. Gladstone wanted him to be his successor, but he ceded to Lord Rosebery. From 1902 he was Leader of the Liberals in the House of Lords. Consuelo, Duchess of Marlborough recalled a visit to the Spencers at Althorp in his latter years: 'Lord Spencer, with his great red beard, his fine head and tall frame, looked every inch a Saxon.' He talked to her about politics and recreated a picture of a lost age. But she found life at Althorp very formal. Four days running, she was invariably seated between her host and the Brazilian Minister, so strictly were the rules of precedence observed. His beautiful wife, known in Dublin as 'Spencer's Faery Queen' was childless.

The Red Earl was not therefore a direct ancestor of Lady Diana, but again an ancestral uncle. He was succeeded in 1910 by his half-brother, Charles Robert, 6th Earl Spencer, KG (1857–1922), known as 'Bobby' Spencer to his friends. He served as Groom-in-Waiting in Queen Victoria's Court in 1886 and then as Vice-Chamberlain from 1892 to 1895. He was Lord Chamberlain to King Edward VII from 1905 until the King's death and then to King George V for a further two years. Sir Frederick Ponsonby, the King's Assistant Private Secretary, found him a difficult man. 'He should not have been, but distinctly was, a snob,' he noted on their visit to Denmark in 1908, 'and resented (Sir Charles) Hardinge going in front of him, a Minister . . .' In Stockholm, Sir Frederick found him complaining that cold beef, cold sausage and cheese was a breakfast for which he had no stomach at such an early hour and later found him in a terrible fuss over the presentation of certain orders and decorations. Clearly the life of the Lord Chamberlain was fraught with many problems in Edwardian times. The 6th Earl died in 1922 and was succeeded by his son, Jack, Lady Diana's grandfather.

Jack, the 7th Earl Spencer, was a prominent Northamptonshire figure and its Lord Lieutenant from 1952 to 1967. Interestingly, his career differed in many respects from those of his ancestors. He served in the Life Guards rather than the Navy and was never a courtier, nor involved in National politics. He was a Conservative, while previous Spencers were invariably Whigs or Liberals. He surpassed all of them in his knowledge and interest in the arts. Much of his time was devoted to arranging, restoring and developing the art treasures at Althorp. He made the Muniment Room there into the best record office in private hands. He moved the 18th century doors and marble chimney pieces designed by John Vardy and 'Athenian' Stuart from Spencer House after the war, as well as bringing the fine 18th century portraits and furniture. He removed eighteen tons of bedroom walls from the first floor of Althorp and then was able to build cases in which to display his superb collection of 18th century Chelsea, Meissen and Sèvres porcelain. He loaned works of art to exhibitions and edited Garrick's letters to Lady Spencer. He was the first of his family to open Althorp to the public.

Just as the war began, Queen Mary lunched at Althorp on her way to take sanctuary at Badminton. James Lees-Milne also paid several visits to Althorp during the war years, while he was employed by the National Trust. He referred to Lord Spencer as 'that difficult

Earl Spencer, with his son and heir, Viscount Althorp, in the cellar of the family home.

nobleman'. Lees-Milne was often the victim of the peppery side of the old Earl's character. He found Lord Spencer 'huffy' when he arrived late one day, 'in evident ill-humour' in the coffee room at Brooks's on another, and when he breakfasted with Lord Spencer in the club in January 1942, he listened to the Earl's 'disgust' at discovering that the contemporary gates at Spencer House, St James's, had been removed for scrap. In August 1943, Lord Spencer took Lees-Milne to see the family's London home. The windows had been blown out, part of the top floor had been destroyed. Lees-Milne noted 'The rooms facing the park on the ground and first floors are very fine, notably the rooms at the south-west corner, one over the other . . . the upper room, now alas badly damaged, was painted by Athenian Stuart . . . There are seventy bedrooms, some very small and poky.' Spencer House is now an office block.

Like the Queen Mother, Lord Spencer sat for Augustus John and the result was characteristically controversial. 'I painted what I saw,' explained John. 'But many people have told me I ought to have been hung instead of the picture.' Lord Spencer was a trustee of the Wallace Collection and a member of the Standing Commission on Museums and Galleries. He was Chairman of the Executive Committee of the Royal School of Needlework and said in 1957: 'Embroidery is the finest relaxation I know – it is as good as a night-cap before one retires after a worrying day.' Because it was so expensive having tapestry chairs repaired professionally he worked on them himself. Thus many of the chairs at Althorp today are examples of his skill.

Lord Spencer died at St Matthew's Nursing Home in Northampton on 9 June 1975, at the age of 85. Lady Diana was then nearly fourteen. In 1969, the Queen Mother had attended the Golden Wedding celebrations of the Spencers in London. In May 1976, after they were both dead, she came to Northampton to open Cynthia Spencer House, the continuing care unit near Mansfield Hospital, a special unit established to provide care for patients suffering from cancer, who require short term or intermittent stays. Lady Diana's father is the present Patron of the Northampton Committee of the House and the Queen Mother lunched at Althorp on the day of her visit.

The bride's father beaming happily after the engagement was announced.

Lady Diana's grandmother, the Countess Spencer, was born in 1897 and died in 1972 after a year's illness. Like Ruth, Lady Fermoy, she was a Dame Commander of the Royal Victorian Order and a Lady of the Bedchamber to the Queen Mother. She was in attendance in 1938 when the King and Queen made their state visit to Paris. She was born Lady Cynthia Hamilton, and her family were always close to the Royal Household. Her father, the 3rd Duke of Abercorn, KG, bore the canopy at the Coronation of King George VI in 1937. He had been Treasurer of King Edward VII's Household from 1903 to 1905. Lady Spencer's sister is Lady Katherine Seymour, DCVO, a Woman of the Bedchamber to the Queen Mother from 1937 to 1960 and now an Extra Woman of the Bedchamber. Their sister-in-law, the present Dowager Duchess of Abercorn, DCVO, has been the Queen Mother's Mistress of the Robes since 1964.

The Countess Spencer was an ardent supporter of many good causes in Northamptonshire, and during the war she was Chairman of the Women's Land Army County Committee for Northamptonshire. After

her death, a friend wrote: 'Her presence was lovely, and she had a very clear intelligence in the service of a remarkably sweet, loyal and sympathetic nature, which won the affectionate admiration of everyone who knew her.' When James Lees-Milne had an informal lunch of poached eggs with maize and cabbage at Althorp in January 1942, he noted: 'Lady Spencer, like a goddess, distilled charm and gentleness around her.'

The 7th Earl Spencer had two sisters, Lady Diana's great aunts, who were Ladies-in-Waiting to the Queen Mother. Lady Delia Peel, who died in January 1981 at the age of 91, was Extra Woman of the Bedchamber and a DCVO. When young, she learned the piano and 'cello and at the Royal College of Music. She was in attendance during the Royal tour of South Africa in 1947, and was a much loved companion for the Queen and Princess Margaret as they grew up. Lady Lavinia Spencer was born in 1899, and the Queen Mother was a bridesmaid at her village wedding to Lord Annaly in 1919. She became an Extra Lady-in-Waiting to the Queen Mother when she was Duchess of York. Lady Annaly accompanied the Yorks on their East African journey of 1924–25 as a companion to the Duchess. Theirs was a lifelong friendship; when Lady Annaly was ill, the Queen Mother paid many visits to her, climbing the high steps up to her Lowndes Square flat. Lady Annaly died in 1955. There is another link, too. Lord Annaly's sister married into the Lowther family, who own Guilsborough Court, Northamptonshire, a house that used to be taken by the Duke of York for hunting in the 1920s. The Queen Mother's close ties with Northamptonshire are long established.

A picture taken at the time of the Golden Wedding of the late Earl and Countess Spencer, Lady Diana's grandparents, 6th March 1969. In the back row, from left to right, are Richard Wake-Walker, Lady Anne Wake-Walker (aunt of the bride), Elizabeth Wake-Walker, Captain Christopher Wake-Walker, Earl and Countess Spencer, the Hon. Sarah Spencer, Viscount Althorp (as he then was), and the Hon. Jane Spencer.
In front are the Hon. Diana Spencer (who became Lady Diana Spencer on the death of her grandfather in 1975), and her brother the Hon. Charles Spencer.

Lady Diana leaves Althorp for a new home in London and another in Gloucestershire. Althorp is an eighteenth century mansion of outstanding interest, but its origins date from the early 1500s. It was then a moated courtyard house, and Sir John Spencer added the forecourt wings in 1575. In the middle of the 17th century the internal courtyard was covered over and became the Grand Staircase. Sir John's son, Sir Robert, decorated the house in the Italian style and John Evelyn noted that the rooms and furnishings were 'such as may become a great prince'. The Long Picture Gallery survives from the days when it was endowed with notable portraits by Van Dyck and Lely. In the days of Mr John Spencer, the Entrance Hall was remodelled, and through the generosity of Sarah, Duchess of Marlborough, Althorp became the home of the famous Marlborough plate, which travelled with the General on his campaign in the Low Countries.

Althorp was extensively repaired in the days of the 2nd Earl, who chose as his architect Henry Holland, who was then at work on Carlton House and the Brighton Pavilion. Sir Joshua Reynolds painted three generations of the family, and the Marlborough Room contains only works by him and by Gainsborough. The Grand Staircase has more portraits, while the Dining Room contains large canvases by Salvator Rosa and Guercino, and the Yellow Drawing Room has four portraits by Rubens. The house is filled with superb French and English furniture, and there is an outstanding collection of Oriental and European porcelain. The bride's father and his second wife have completely rearranged the house and though it is open to the public at times it is still lived in as a family home.

The Prince of Wales will now leave Buckingham Palace for a London home of his own. In the summer of 1980 he announced that he no longer still wished to live at Chevening and instead the Duchy of Cornwall purchased Highgrove House, near Tetbury in Gloucestershire for a

Highgrove House, near Tetbury in Gloucestershire, which will be the home of the Prince and Princess of Wales.

sum believed to be in the region of £730,000. The house was previously the home of Mr Maurice Macmillan, the Conservative MP and son of the former Prime Minister, Harold Macmillan.

Highgrove House is eight miles from Gatcombe Park, the home of Princess Anne and Captain Mark Phillips. It is convenient for hunting, which the Prince has come to enjoy in recent years, and well situated for polo at Cirencester and racing at Newbury and Chepstow. (The Prince has now entered the world of steeple-chasing with some success.) The house was advertised for sale as: 'A distinguished Georgian house, standing in superb parkland in the Duke of Beaufort's Hunt. Entrance Hall, four principal reception rooms, domestic quarters, nine bedrooms, six bathrooms, nursery wing. Full central heating. Fine stable block. Easily maintained gardens. Lodge. Farm manager's house. Pair of farm cottages. Dairy unit and farm buildings. In all about 347 acres.'

The wedding of Prince Charles will be the first of a Prince of Wales since that of Albert Edward (the future Edward VII) in 1863. The business of preparing for the great ceremony involves many people. The Lord Chamberlain compiles the guest list and masterminds the entire operation. The Master of the Household arranges the wedding breakfast. The Registrar of St Paul's Cathedral oversees arrangements for the service. The immediate family of the bride and groom will sign the register at the Cathedral during the ceremony, while other members of the Royal Family will sign it at the Palace. Less officially, but no less importantly, the television networks, the radio stations and the souvenir makers spring to life to satisfy the popular demand. There have to be many meetings and probably numerous headaches before the wedding procession of carriages and the Household Cavalry can ride down the Mall.

The Queen said at the time of her Silver Wedding in November 1972: 'A marriage begins by joining man and wife together, but this relationship between two people, however deep at the time, needs to develop and mature with the passing years. For that it must be held firm in the web of family relationships between parents and children, between cousins, aunts and uncles.' We know that Prince Charles wanted to choose his bride with care. This he told us in 1969. He is indeed fortunate to have found in Lady Diana Spencer, somebody who is, in his words, 'pretty special'.

The Prince of Wales gave Lady Diana a sapphire and diamond engagement ring on Sunday, 20th February. At first, she had to keep it secret, but two days later was proudly displaying it to the world's press in the garden of Buckingham Palace.